D1346463

991043920 4

THE HEART OF INDIA

DUNCAN FORBES

The Heart of
INDIA

*Illustrated
and with maps*

ROBERT HALE · LONDON

© Duncan Forbes 1968

First published in Great Britain October 1968

Reprinted February 1969

SBN 7091 0408 1

Robert Hale & Company
63 Old Brompton Limited
London S.W.7

PRINTED IN GREAT BRITAIN
BY EBENEZER BAYLIS AND SON, LTD.
THE TRINITY PRESS, WORCESTER, AND LONDON

CONTENTS

ILLUSTRATIONS

PREFACE

I first went to India in 1941 by troopship round the Cape of Good Hope. It was a wartime voyage to a country about which I knew and cared little. Indeed my ideas about what to expect, as far as I remember them, were juvenile in the extreme. I vaguely imagined that there would be jungles and mountains, maharajas riding on elephants, cavaliers in great green turbans, towering temples, white-robed priests and dancing-girls. I still remember the shock I got when we sat waiting in the train in the dockyard siding in Bombay, and the beggars gathered round, and when we went up into Central India through the night and the next day, and the dry dust and decrepitude and poverty seemed never ending.

Although I was soon to command a hundred men, I was not yet twenty-one, and for the next four impressionable years pictures were printed on my mind that have never left it. They were impressions that built up a kind of love hate relationship, a sort of fascinated repulsion that the thought of India always brings back to me. After I had gone home at the end of the war, I never expected to return there. Yet that repellent fascination still remained.

Even when I was in Malaya, I did not expect to make the journey back there across the Bay of Bengal, and when I left the Venerable Maha Samarn by the huge reclining Buddha in Penang, and he talked of taking his next party of pilgrims to India to see the places where the Buddha was born and lived and died, I never thought that I, myself, would be able to make my own pilgrimage so soon.

But it was so. Two years later I had to visit the Gurkha Recruiting Depots just over the Indian border in Nepal to inspect the schools there and to run a refresher course for the Nepali teachers, and so the ideal opportunity arose to fulfil a long ambition and see those places on the way.

Furthermore I had also to visit the principal English language secondary schools in Darjeeling in order to see whether they were suitable for the children of British Army personnel living at the Depots, and consequently I was able to return there after an absence of twenty years and compare the actuality with my memories.

The lucky chance of my return to Malaya being held up by a delayed aircraft gave me the time and the chance to visit the famous Black and White Pagodas of Orissa, which had always seemed to me to be the most fantastic monuments of the Hindu world.

In 1967 I was back in India again, just after the General Election, this time on a private trip to visit friends in the south of India and to see that part of the country south from Bombay that I had not been to in all the wartime years I had spent in the Indian Army. I wanted to see with my own eyes whether it bore any resemblance to the descriptions I had heard in those days, for the southern part of the peninsula, with its waving palm trees and dark skinned people, has often been described as the "true India" and I felt that not knowing it my knowledge was somehow incomplete.

This book is a record of these journeys, which opened my eyes to the reality of India of the present day set amongst the ruins of its past.

I

IN THE FOOTSTEPS OF THE BUDDHA

WHEN I boarded an Air India Boeing 707 at Paya Lebar airport, Singapore with 169 Gurkha soldiers and their families, who were going home on pension and on leave, it was with a sense of apprehension and curiosity that I set out again for the land that I had not visited for so long. As we flew off north-west up the Malacca Strait, these sturdy, stocky warriors sat six in a row, with a gay wall-paper of palaces and peacocks at their sides and soft music in their ears, whilst the elegant air hostesses, entwined in their saris, served them a midday meal of curry and rice.

The plain of lower Burma passed below, golden with the winter harvest, then sea again, and darkness was with us as we descended over the straggling lights of Calcutta and landed at Dum Dum seven miles out of town. The palaver of customs followed, after which the Gurkhas were transported to the Transit Camp at Barrackpore, prior to being sent off on their various trains, whilst I went into the city with the officer who had come to meet me, giving the obliging customs officials a lift back with us after their work was done.

All the sights and smells of Mother India seemed to come up to meet me during that drive into Calcutta. My companion did not drive himself, as he reckoned that there would be so much trouble if he ever had an accident, even if he were blameless, that it was too risky to do so. Therefore it was his Bengali driver who banged us into and out of the ruts in the road, past the rattling lorries and creaking bullock-carts, and through the crowds of men in dirt white dhotis, who moved through the clouds of acrid white smoke that came from the cow dung cooking fires in the huts by the road.

As we came into the urban heart of the great city, the crowds of dark, lean men in their dim white clothes grew denser. They were packed together up the narrow side streets and in the entrances to the dark hovels like white rats crawling in a complicated maze. The swollen city seemed to fester and groan with the weight of its people, and only after we emerged into the relative spaciousness of Old Court House Street and Chowringhi did there appear to be room to breathe again.

I was glad that I had not got to spend more than a night in that unlovely city, for it was as far removed from the places I wanted to see as a stagnant marsh is from a running stream. Job Charnock and the merchants of the East India Company, who established their trading settlement at the end of the seventeenth century on the flat bank of the River Hooghly, can hardly have had any idea that they were founding a metropolis. It was simply a firm river bank in the midst of a watery wilderness, where pilgrims were wont to disembark on their way to the nearby temple of Kali, from which the city takes its name.

In those days all goods went up into India by water on the great rivers and came out the same way. As often as not men used the same means and were just as likely to take a boat to Benares or Allahabad as to seaports like Madras, for land travel was arduous and dangerous unless one could afford a mounted retinue. So it was simply a place for storage and transhipment, and yet it grew to be the second largest city in the Commonwealth.

In 1696 a fort was built there and named after King William. It flourished until 1756, when it was attacked by Suraj-ud-Daula, and those who did not escape down river were imprisoned in the Black Hole. After the battle of Plassey in the following year a bigger and better Fort William was constructed to the south of the earlier defences at a cost of £2,000,000, which was a very large sum of money in those days. From then on the place just grew and grew, with the population doubling and redoubling itself faster and faster in a kind of fantastic geometrical progression of increase. At the beginning of the nineteenth century there were about 200,000 people there, and Calcutta was already the capital of the whole of British India with a supreme court and a cathedral. By the middle of the century the number was 400,000. It had reached a million by the end of the century and passed 2,000,000 in the first quarter of the twentieth century, even though Delhi had become the capital in 1911. With the assistance of the refugees from Pakistan, it went well past the 3,000,000 mark before the middle of the twentieth century.

As I walked out of my hotel into the crowded streets I wondered where this frightening evidence of the power of the terrible goddess Kali would finally lead to, for Kali is the *shakti*, or female energy, of Siva, the reproducer, and unless the tide of reproduction ceases to flood, semi-starvation and squalor would seem to be the pre-destined lot of masses of the people. It is of all the cities of India the most crowded and the most squalid. The large open space of the *maidan*, with Government House and other noble buildings of an earlier age at the city end of it, and the Victoria memorial, Curzon's

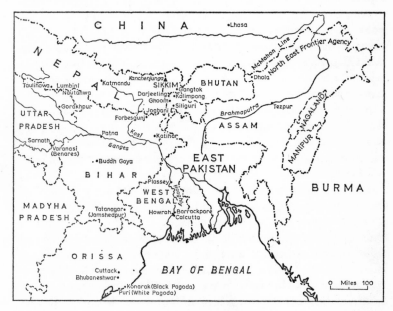

Eastern India

grandiloquent monument to the Indian Empire, at the far end, only accentuates by contrast the sordid misery of the pullulating streets.

One is greeted by beggars at the very threshold of one's hotel. They come running up, brandishing their stumps of arms and withered hands, pointing at their sightless eyes and speechless mouths, showing off their flapping bellies and shrivelled dugs. In London one would be shocked to the core at such a sight. It would be unbelievable. But here it somehow seems to be a natural part of the scene. One expected it to be just as one saw it twenty years ago, for in India, in spite of the fine talk and the atomic reactors, things do not change. Life to the average man is such a frightening and hopeless combination of penury and insecurity that the only way to support it is to regard it as an illusion, as a short, wretched interlude between the life past and the life to come.

It was in some such sort that I regarded Calcutta during my brief stay there, for it was hardly to be credited that real men, women and children were living in this day and age in such vile abjectness, or that the creatures sleeping on the broad pavement in front of my hotel were real creatures.

Next day I walked out on to the street in a kind of daze and was passed from beggar to beggar, each of whom had a separate segment of pavement. Money changers vied with them for my attention. A thick smell, compounded of crude tobacco and the burning strings which save the customers the expense of buying matches, came from the tobacconists' booths. There was a woman washing under a fire hydrant. Seven thin men, carrying a cupboard on their heads, walked past, an eighth thin man, tinkling a bell like an ironic jester's motley, pulled his rickshaw across the road in my direction. Another man strolled by stark naked except for a silver sword stuck through his foreskin.

I turned away from him and almost into the arms of a money changer's tout, a handsome youth with white shirt tails flapping over a pair of pyjamas, who lured me into the New Market to do a deal with Singapore dollars at the free exchange rate. Closely followed by a uniformed and numbered porter, who hoped to carry my eventual purchases, I entered the covered ways, which smelt of incense and sandalwood, of sweetmeats and bags of brown sugar.

In the Bengal Souvenir Shop the proprietor had just returned from worship at Kalighat, one and a half miles away. He had brought back bright clay idols of Ganesh, the elephant headed god of luck, and of Lakshmi, the goddess of wealth, in a bed of flower petals, for it was New Year's day, and I was lucky to find him there, he said, as most shops were closed.

So the least I could do was to change my money with him, and with my wad of rupees I threaded my way out of the market into the street again, still followed by the disappointed porter number 40, who had no purchases to carry.

As I walked back to the hotel a Mr Mukherjee got into conversation with me. He was a greying, courteous man and told me he was a shipping supervisor in Bombay, Madras and Calcutta, showing me his card to prove it. We passed a devotee of Siva with ashen body, matted hair, white lines on his forehead, a metal trident and a human skull, far surpassing in grime the roughest of the beatniks and the provos. "They should not come into the towns," said Mr Mukherjee. "They belong to the villages. But they come for food. There are too many people, so there is not enough food." He smiled at having made such a neat equation. A burly storehouse watchman shook out a gunny bag, throwing a cloud of floury dust into our faces. "Ignorant peoples," said Mr Mukherjee. "Nobody tells them what to do." He smiled again at the success of his explanation. "Excuse me," he said, as he began to try the inevitable touch for a loan.

The haunted look of the Indians in the jammed trams, in the aluminium buses and in the melancholy black horse-cabs followed me as I went down to Howrah station, after surprising the hotel cashier, who did not think that his guests ought to travel by any means other than air. As far as he was concerned the No. 5 Up, Amritsar Mail, belonged to a past order of things. Nevertheless it was waiting there on platform 8, it left Howrah at the correct time, and it rumbled across the Ganges on the long Dufferin bridge into Benares at 9.15 next morning to deliver me at the first stage of my pilgrimage.

I had previously breakfasted off two tiny hardboiled eggs, toast and pale butter, served on the chipped crockery of the Indian Railways, during a long wait at Kashi, the station for the old town, whilst watching certain citizens dusting off patches of platform with the ends of their blanket rolls in order to clear spaces on which to lie down, so there was no need to delay. I went off immediately to Sarnath, the goal of my thoughts.

It is here, four miles north of the city that the deer park was situated, in which Sakyamuni Buddha preached his first and subsequent sermons. The name "Sarang Nath" means "Deer Lord," and confused thinking and reminiscences, no doubt, of Siva in the form of a deer, have led some people to say that the Buddha himself appeared here as a deer. Such a magical transformation is quite out of character, however, for there is no real evidence that the Buddha ever left his human form during his lifetime. After he had found enlightenment at Buddh Gaya, a hundred miles to the east, he came to Sarnath to preach a sane and rational creed of peace as a human being.

And indeed, after the mad turmoil of Calcutta the whole atmosphere of Sarnath seemed to be one of peace and sanity. During the heyday of Buddhism in India it had been the site of a large monastery, and there were also lofty memorial stupas as well as the stone pillar set up by the Emperor Asoka, who converted India to Buddhism. But after a thousand years Buddhism finally withered away in the land of its birth, having surrendered to the weird and exciting extravagances of medieval Hindu practices. Sarnath became deserted. The buildings fell into ruin, and little but the two big stupas remained above ground. One of these, the Darmarajika Stupa, or stupa of the "King of the Law", was partially demolished by the prime minister of a raja of Benares for the sake of the bricks of which it was made. He showed the way to a crowd of early nineteenth-century treasure seekers, who carried away what relics they could turn up out of the ground.

Nevertheless modern excavations initiated by General Cunningham in the late nineteenth century and directed by the Archaeological Department of the Government of India have revealed the outlines of the monastery area, of the raised plinth on which the Buddha is said to have preached, and of the main shrine containing numerous small memorial stupas. The stump of the Asoka pillar is there, with its inscription warning monks against schisms, whilst its capital of four lions back to back, superimposed above a circular motif of a lion, a bull, an elephant and a horse, with four wheels in between, stands in the museum. It is a beautiful work in polished sandstone, and it is little wonder that it was adopted as the symbol of the new Republic of India.

The site is beautifully laid out, with lawns between the stone walks and walls that looked surprisingly green in the dry heat of April. Dominating the whole area stands the big Dhamekh ("Pondering the Law") stupa. Some of the lavish geometrical carving of its high stone plinth remains, although the eight niches for the statues of the Buddha are empty.

The peace of all this is, of course, the peace of the dead, but on one side of the deer park there is a building that is still alive. It is the temple built by the Mahabodhi Society of India, Japan and Ceylon in 1931 in the style of the ancient Mahabodh temple at Gaya. Its walls are decorated from top to bottom with vivid frescoes done in the Ajanta style by a team of Japanese artists in 1936. They represent scenes from the Buddha's life, starting with a picture of him sitting in the Tusita heaven before his birth on earth, and finishing with his last long sleep. In the middle the great scene of his victory over the temptations of Mara and his daughters is depicted. Strangely enough the paintings were commissioned by a British Buddhist, Mr B. L. Broughton.

Beside the temple stands a pale green Aswatha tree, transplanted as a sapling from Ceylon also in 1931. It is a descendant of the original Bodhi tree at Gaya, under which the Buddha found enlightenment. Nearby there is a real deer park with live deer in it, whilst across the road a number of viharas and dharmsalas for pilgrims have been built.

Most of the visitors come from abroad—from Thailand, Burma and Ceylon, where Buddhism of the Theravada school, the Doctrine of the Elders, still thrives. As Christians go from Europe to the holy places in Palestine, so South-east Asians go to Uttar Pradesh, the Northern Province of India, to see the cradle of Buddhism. They go to Lumbini, the birthplace of the Buddha, to Buddh Gaya, the place of his enlightenment, to Sarnath, the centre of his ministry, and to Kusinara, where he died. Nor are the visitors backward or out of date. Thai monks thought nothing of flying by jet airliner to India in 1966 with nine stone spheres, covered with gold leaf, to be set in the foundations of their new temple at Gaya. The stream of the doctrine was simply flowing back to its source.

After the peace of Sarnath I plunged back into the whirlpool of illusion, following a brief air-conditioned interlude in Clark's hotel. An Ambassador car, one of the three types now made in India, and sister to the Hindustan and the Roadmaster, took me from the cantonment of British Empire days into the city of Benares, which has now reverted to its older name of Varanasi, after the River Varna and the Asi stream, between which it lies on the west bank of the Ganges.

Hardly another car was to be seen, and those few that there were had to thread their way through a ringing throng of tricycles. Tumbledown houses were interspersed with open areas of wasteland that looked like bomb sites, and in another country one would have assumed that the city was still recovering from a vicious airraid. But then one knew that the Indian cities always had looked like this, that the bricks they were built of were always pale, crumbling and sunbaked, that the wooden posts and beams would never feel a drop of paint, that the potholes in the roads would never be

2

filled in, and that with their cows, goats, chickens, earth and dust
they would still be essentially just overgrown villages.

On the southern fringe of this hotchpotch of human and animal
life lies the red Durga temple, which was built in the eighteenth
century by a woman of Bengal, the Rani of Natore. It is dedicated
to a woman too, for Durga is another name for Siva's consort,
Kali, in her terrifying form of lust and destructiveness, a delighter
in animal sacrifices.

Monkeys outnumbered the human beings there. Down below,
worshippers moved across the courtyard, but the monkeys cared
nothing of this as they leaped and swung on the red tower and on
the raised ambulatory on which I was standing. Black faced lemurs
were prominent among them. Their long tails were tipped with
black because, as Hanuman, the monkey god, they had used them as
firebrands in the assault of the castle of the demon king of Ceylon.

The temple custodian's boy kept them at bay with a stick longer
than his own height, and I solved the problems of baksheesh by
giving him a promissory note, called a "temple tip", as provided for
tourists by the hotel. Meanwhile the worshipping women, with their
brass trays of offerings, continued their devotions oblivious to their
surroundings. The temple bell, presented by "Mister William
James Grant Sahib Bahadur, Collector of Benares" in 1808 in
gratitude for his family's rescue from a whirlpool in the great
Ganges, rang out three times. A monkey tapped me on the arm to
attract my attention, asking for a tasty tip.

This was a good spot from which to begin a visit to the ghats, or
stone terraces, which line the west bank of the holy river from the
Asi to the Varna. There are nearly fifty of them, all carefully
demarcated, some private, some public, some allotted to a particular
Hindu sect, some set aside for cremations, for this is precious land
beside the immortal river. Yet the opposite bank, subject to in-
undations, is virtually untouched by man and remains an open
bare expanse.

Of all these ghats there are five which the earnest pilgrim should
visit and bathe from in a single day, and of these five the most
important is in the middle—the Dasaswamedh Ghat. The words
mean the ghat of the Ten Horse Sacrifice. Such an offering would
have been precious indeed to the ancient Aryan cavaliers, and thus
Brahma made the place equal in sanctity to the great confluence of
the Ganges and the Jumna further upstream.

I went down to this ghat along the narrow street that leads to it from the town, as the only way I could have reached it along the waterfront would have been by boat. There is no continuous riverside promenade. In some places great blocks of stone have fallen down the crumbling bank, blocking the path, and in others private owners, mindful only of their own families' bliss in their next reincarnations, deny the right of way.

I walked down the steps past the stacks of little earthenware pots, in which the holy water is taken home, and faced the broad river, which at this point still has seven or eight hundred miles to go to reach the sea. The Brahmin holy men were sitting about under their umbrellas and bamboo shelters. I walked down to the bottom step. It was true that the water, flowing over the sandy river bed, looked clear and unpolluted, yet I did not care to drink.

Instead, I walked downstream past barges laden with the stone blocks and boulders that were being used for restoration of the river bank. I went up another alleyway from the Lalita Ghat to visit the Nepalese temple. Built of red brick and black wood, with double overhanging roofs in the style of the pagodas of Katmandu, it is unique in Benares. It stands on a secluded terrace above the river, and like its Katmandu models, it is embellished with erotic carvings.

The pujari, who lives in a little house beside the temple courtyard, told me he received a stipend of eight rupees a month, and showed me photographs of the King and Queen of Nepal, the Crown Prince and the late King Tribhubana in his front porch. He indicated Kamadeva, the Hindu Eros, at the gateway, and was at pains to point out the details of the coupled figures in the eaves. Inside, in the centre of the building, stood the generative engine, the stone phallus, with an earthenware pot hanging above it, from which water dripped to keep it, symbolically, from overheating. The temple must have considerable importance for Nepalese royalty, who have, in the past, always chosen Benares to live in whenever they have had to go into exile from their own country.

I went back to the ghat, and a little further downstream I passed a wall painted white, with the following words written on it: MALARIA WORKER YOUR FRIEND. GIVE HIM CO-OPERATION. There I came upon some women, who were slapping cowdung on to another wall. It was passed up to them in wet cakes by their daughters, who were at the bottom of the ladders on which they were standing. Just beyond them there were large stacks of wood, for this was the fuel store of the Jalsain Ghat, where large numbers of cremations take place all the year round.

The background to the ghat is a conglomeration of towers and spires, belonging, strangely enough, to mosques as well as temples, for Islam has also left its stamp on this Hindu holy place. It is against this backdrop of grey stone interspersed with gold that the bodies are burnt.

I saw two fires that were near to ashes and another that was still blazing merrily. Two corpses—one wrapped in white and the other in red—lay on the steps with their feet to the river, whilst Ganges water was being sprinkled on them. Another body was being carried down to join them. Just below me a man with his head freshly shaven, except for the single knotted Brahminical tuft, was getting into a clean white shift, preparing for his duties as chief mourner. He was presumably the son or nearest male relative of the deceased.

Suddenly there was a hideous crackle and rattle of bones. The wild haired attendant of a funeral pyre had whipped a corpse off the embers, which was not quite consumed, and knocked it with his long stave into the water. The river hissed and steamed. The body remained there, close to the bank, with a rump of red meat breaking the surface. A dog ran forward to sniff at it. The mourners murmured, then hurried away. Yet they still say Ganges water is as pure as heaven. Jalsain, who is Vishnu as the Sleeper on the Ocean, watches over it.

From the nearby Lalita Ghat I left the river bank and went up a narrow tunnel towards the Golden temple, creeping past cows and more women making fuel cakes out of their dung. It stands in the midst of a confusing mass of narrow streets, facing the large mosque of Alamgir, and I was allowed to go up on to the balcony of a house facing the entrance. From here I could see the three towers, including the two famous golden ones, which were gilded at the expense of Ranjit Sing, the Lion of the Punjab. Warren Hastings, one presumes more out of policy than religious fervour, paid for the music gallery.

In fact this shrine, like many of the noted centres of the Hindu faith, is not very old. It was built in the middle of the eighteenth century, during the upsurge of Hinduism which came about after power had passed from the Muslim rulers to the East India Company. It is not even as old as the mosque of Alamgir, whose white domes I could see beyond the cigar shaped towers of the temple. The Hindus complained that the Emperor Aurangzeb had destroyed their ancient holy place in the early eighteenth century, but even that only dated back to a little over a hundred years before.

There they stood, cheek by jowl, these two antitheses of faith that racked India for centuries in greater or lesser outbursts until the last great holocaust of slaughter in 1947. The Hindu is polytheist, sensual, complicated, rioting in the imagination; the Muslim monotheist, austere, simple and disciplined. The mosque, which I later passed on foot, was deserted, as the Muslim population, which includes the weavers of the beautiful Benares silk brocades, has dwindled. But there was a steady stream of people going in and out of the temple, and the alley was strewn with fallen petals of jasmine and hibiscus.

After giving another "temple tip" to the smooth Brahmin in charge of the visitors to the balcony, I went down into the crowded bazaar, and out of all the shops displaying brass and ivory ware I bought two beans, each one with six ivory elephants in it. At the Oriental Arts Factory in Maqbal Alam road, however, it was not so easy to get away. After seeing the master craftsmen and apprentice boys working the silks on their wooden looms, and being fanned vigorously by one of the boys, and having a stick of incense lit in front of me, and receiving a morsel of gold thread, and accepting a Green Spot orange juice, and seeing the photographs of Mrs Kennedy, the President's widow, I felt in all conscience bound to buy a stole or at least a headscarf.

Then I set off again, this time in the No. 76 passenger train bound for Gorakhpur. It was a slow overnight journey on the metre gauge, and the cool breeze, though welcome, covered everything in smuts from the engine. We passed the red rectangular buildings of the Gurkha recruiting depot at Kunraghat in the pale light of the false dawn, and reached our destination at 5.30 a.m.

Even at this unearthly hour the station waiting room, which seemed to be used as a free hotel by the local officials, was crowded. A Sikh was carefully binding on his blue turban and enclosing his beard in a muslin bag, whilst a fat captain of the Railway Police, clad in khaki trousers and an open bushjacket, was folding up his bedding roll. A Brahmin, with the tips of his fingers together, holding his string brahminical thread, was sitting crosslegged yogi fashion, saying his prayers.

As I started my English breakfast with soft cornflakes and warm buffalo milk, I read some of the strange items of news that one sees in Indian newspapers. In one place a group of people had been accused of attempting to injure the prime minister by means of the magical symbolism of a Tantric Yojna, in another a keen school staff had put on a fire-fighting display in order to impress a visiting education officer—and burnt to death the schoolboy who was acting as guinea pig.

Only thirty-four miles to the east of Gorakhpur lie the ruins of the Monastery of the Great Decease at Kusinara. Here, where the Buddha died, is located the huge reclining image of the dying Buddha, which is the original of the one I knew in Penang. There is also an enormous seated Buddha, as well as the remains of many buildings and stupas together with modern dharmsalas to house the pilgrims from Burma and Thailand.

Leaving Kusinara behind, I went on to the border of Nepal to visit my last place of pilgrimage, which should have been the first. It was the birthplace of the Buddha at Lumbini.

Wind and dust were blowing up as the little train pulled out of Gorakhpur for Nautanwa, past a collection of vintage steam locomotives that would have gladdened the heart of a railway enthusiast. It moved slowly along its embankment across the bare harvested fields, whilst I watched the movement of white egrets and blue kingfishers over the flat plain. Then it stopped for no apparent reason. A man got out to relieve himself beside the line and was nearly left behind as we started off again.

With work in the fields finished until the rains the stations were crowded with people on the move, the men haunted and wild eyed and the women passive in their big chunky silver anklets, their toe rings, nose rings, ear pendants and chokers of chain link jewellery. It was not surprising, therefore, that we reached the Nautanwa railhead an hour late. A Land-Rover from the Recruiting Centre of the British Brigade of Gurkhas at Paklihawa on the Nepalese side of the border was there to meet me, and it was under the hospitable arrangements of the Officer Commanding, Major Alistair Langlands, that I was able to make my pilgrimage the following day.

I set out from my tented accommodation in another Land-Rover, heading northwards towards the large Nepalese village of Bhairewa. At last the foothills of the Himalayas could be seen in a long line across the plain, but after a mile or so we turned off to the left down a deeply rutted track, which we had to follow in a south-westerly direction for sixteen miles.

It was sad to see venerable groves of peepul trees being slaughtered to feed the brickyard kilns at several places along the route, and it seemed to be the ultimate stage in the reduction of fertile lands to desert plain, which has been taking place in so many places in India ever since the peasants were allowed to cut down the forests in the springtide of nineteenth-century liberalism. But blessedly, although bridges were in disrepair and one had actually fallen down, the countryside through which we passed had not yet been quite reduced to a treeless expanse. There were monkeys, and there was much bird life, including ospreys, kingfishers and green pigeons, and as we followed a train of creaking bullock carts up from the river ford, I saw one of the large grey-backed, red-beaked secretary birds.

We left the carters shouting at their oxen and prodding at their humps to spur them to further effort, and drove on along the track. As well as the driver there were three young Gurkha soldiers with me, who had come along for the ride, although they were not quite sure what they were going to see. One of them shouted out to announce our arrival, when from behind an intervening patch of rising ground two hemispherical stupas, surmounted by brick pillars, appeared. The stupas are old, but the pillars of brick, looking like the chimneys one sometimes sees emerging from the hillside over railway tunnels in England, are recent innovations of one of the maharajas of Nepal.

We crossed the last primitive bridge, bumping up and down six inch gaps between the road surface and the baulks of timber of which it was constructed, skirted a barbed wire fence, and entered the hallowed precincts of Lumbini, after first removing the broken panel of a gate.

It was an empty, quiet place. Facing us stood the new white pillar, standing in a lotus and surrounded by a circle of seats for the weary, which was erected by the present King of Nepal to commemorate a recent Buddhist convention. On one side there was an old lodging house for pilgrims and on the other a new temple, built in a mixture of the Indian and Nepalese style, whilst in the centre, rooted in magnificent isolation, lay an old steamroller, sunk deep into the ground.

The saffron robed bhikku showed us over the temple, pointing out the marble Buddha from Rangoon and its inscription, which he was able to translate as at one time he had lived in Burma. My

Gurkha boys were most interested in all this, and although nominally Hindus they put their cash into the offertory most willingly. They were equally happy to pay up their paisa at the whitewashed shrine, which is the centre of the real antiquities of the place, for no doubt they felt themselves to be in the presence of great and wonderful things.

In fact these antiquities consist of three things. Firstly, within the shrine, which is on a platform some six feet above the plain, there is a statue. It is a portrayal in medium relief on a flat base, about half life size, of a woman with her hand upraised holding on to the branch of a tree, and a baby, already on its feet, beside her. This represents the birth of the Buddha. It has been represented thus elsewhere in various representations in stone of the life of the Buddha, but the reasons that lead us to believe that this is indeed the true and actual place where this great event took place are too strong to be denied. The facts are that here the statue, undoubtedly very old, is on its own and not one of a series, and furthermore the spot coincides closely with where we must suppose the place to be from a careful reading of the Buddhist canon. Finally the Emperor Asoka, living much closer to the event in the third century B.C., was clearly convinced that it was here. But let us hear the story:

When she was forty-five Queen Maya, the principal wife of Suddhodhana, King of the Sakyas, had a dream. She dreamt that she saw a spotless white elephant with a white lotus in its trunk entering her womb. When the dream was recounted to the learned Brahmins, they said that it meant she had conceived and would give birth to a male child. On learning this the king rejoiced, for he had no heir.

And so it happened. The queen became pregnant. According to legend in the later months of her pregnancy her skin became so transparent that the child could actually be seen within her womb. When her time was drawing near, Queen Maya expressed a desire to leave the palace at Kapilavastu and go to her father's house in Devadaha for her confinement. So she set out in a golden palanquin. She had got as far as Lumbini grove when she saw the sal trees in full bloom, and asked her bearers to stop there for a rest. She stretched up her hand to catch hold of a particular bough, laden with blooms, that had caught her fancy, and as she did so she gave birth to her child cleanly and painlessly. The Buddha stood up immediately, and took seven steps towards the north. The steps are shown in the carving as footprints on lotus blooms.

That is the story. Now the ruins of Kapilavastu have been uncovered at Taulihawa fifteen miles to the west of Lumbini, and in addition the name of Lumbini or Lummini was preserved down the ages with so little change that it has been known as Rummindei right up to the present time.

The second piece of evidence is the split pillar with parts of a blackened capital that stands beside the shrine, protected by a modern iron railing. It can be no other than the pillar which the Chinese pilgrim, Hiuen Tsang, saw in the seventh century A.D. and described as having been spilt by lightning, for it is one of the pillars erected by Asoka, who was also called Piyadasi, on various important sites in his empire. The translation of the Pali inscription, which though worn by time, can still easily be deciphered, reads thus:

> King Piyadasi, the beloved of the Devas, in the twentieth year of his reign, himself made a royal visit. Sakyamuni Buddha having been born here, a stone railing was built and a stone pillar erected. The Lord having been born here, Lummini village was freed of tax and entitled to the eighth part.

Thirdly, near the shrine and the pillar lies the square pond, or tanks as such stretches of water are called in India, with partly excavated brick walls around it. "The water is warm in winter and cool in summer," my driver told me. Surely this must be where Maya bathed after giving birth.

If more evidence were needed, it would be the object discovered by Mr Peppé, the former owner of the estate round his own village of Peppégunj, which was the name of one of the crowded stations I had passed through on my way up to the railhead. Digging into one of the stupas in 1898, he found a casket with an inscription on it, which was interpreted as saying, "This reliquary of the Divine Buddha is that of the Sakyas." The sentence clearly refers to the division into eight parts of the relics of the Buddha after his cremation at Kusinara.

So there is little doubt that the great teacher, whose wisdom in one form or another went hand in hand with civilization all over the Far East, was born here at Lumbini. But in the land of his birth in the course of time he came to be either forgotten or honoured simply as one of the many deities of the Hindu pantheon. After that it was not until this century that any attention at all was paid to this remote part of the borderlands of Nepal and the Northern Province of India, in the lee of the Himalayas.

And it is still remote. Except on the special occasions of religious gatherings few people go there. When I was there, I saw no other visitors besides my party of three Gurkha boys and a Nepalese driver. A big tree hangs over the shrine and tank, but the rest of the grove is gone and attempts to replant it have not met with success. In all the open fields round about one feels an air of nostalgia for the noble happenings of the distant past that took place in this ancient Buddha land. But far from the fret and tension of the modern world there is also peace. The steamroller stuck in the centre of nothingness is a symbol of our own times, which under eternity will go down like the rest. Over the plains, here and there, one sees the low mounds that conceal the ruins of a once populous land and still await the archaeologist.

I went back to Paklihawa by the same route as I had come, and drove into the smart military camp, that contrasted sharply with the straggle of huts and tracks round about, where the camp followers lived. At the threshold of my tent a small, grave group awaited. The washerman presented me with my clean shirt, held out on both his palms as if it were a precious cloth of gold, the watercarrier awaited the word *ghusl* to go off and bring back his cans of hot and cold water and pour them into the zinc bathtub, my personal servant, still called a bearer from his former duties of carrying the sahib in his palanquin, wanted to know what clothes I would wear for dinner, and the gardener offered me a posy of marigolds.

This was the old life of India, with the retinue of serious and courteous servants in feudal relationship of lord and vassal, which I had known so many years before that it seemed to be in a previous incarnation. The *dhobi* and the *bheesti* and the *mali* dispersed, leaving me alone with the bearer, who spoke of Lehra, about twenty miles away, where he had previously worked before the British Gurkha depot was moved into Nepal.

"Lehra," he said. "Station Bridgemangunj. Very close to here. That is where Bridgeman Sahib used to have his estates. The Company gave him all the jungle as far as he could see—eighteen miles. It was for his bravery. Seven *kosh* one way and seven *kosh* the other. And he cut it down to grow indigo. Then after that he grew sugar. There were five parts of it, and Walsh Sahib used to look after them. Now all gone *phut. Dunya kharab hogaya.* The world has gone bad."

He spoke of these things as though they had happened only yesterday, but Bridgeman died over a hundred years ago, and the Company he talked about was the East India Company, which handed over its affairs to the British Government in the 1860s. Thus the folk memory of the people persists, and each generation talks of things in history as though they had happened in its own time.

The *bheesti* returned with the water, and I stepped into my tub. I thought of the two British officers living in this place, who were my hosts—the Commanding Officer and the Paymaster. They could hardly have been living further away from their own kind, and one might have supposed that they would sometimes kick at the exile in which they had been placed.

Nothing could have been further from the truth. Both of them wished for nothing better than to be left in their appointments there indefinitely, enjoying the parochial world of the Indian countryside, the distinctions of rank, the mutual respect between superior and inferior, the talk of the land and the seasons, the big game and the wild fowl, with an occasional visitor by rail from Gorakhpur or by plane from Katmandu to break the spell.

As I sat in my zinc tub with the smell of a damp concrete floor, of canvas and shoepolish, of the neem tree and the magnolia in my nostrils, I thought of another man I had known, who wanted nothing greater in life than this.

THE HILL STATION

A FORTNIGHT later I recrossed the frontier of Nepal into Bihar 300 miles further east, and caught another train at Jogbani for a slow ride of four and a half hours to the main line at Katihar. Apart from the delicious lychees on sale at the wayside stations there was little to recommend it. For five minutes I had a personal reason for awakened interest when we stopped at Forbesgunj, but I was sorry to see someone urinating on the platform of the station that carried my name.

At Katihar I joined the Assam Mail, and travelled with an Indian Air Force flight-lieutenant and his wife coming from Allahabad, a jemadar of the Indian Grenadiers and a "no ticket" passenger sitting on the step of the carriage. The scenery on the flat plain was much the same as it had been on the first stage of the journey—mud and wattle villages, a few fields being ploughed with shallow wooden ploughshares, occasionally a long-legged crane standing by the bank of a stream.

After a meal of curry and rice we reached Siliguri. It was already after 10 p.m., but there was still a three-and-a-half-hour drive by car, for I was bound for Darjeeling, the hill-station of Bengal, which was 50 miles and 7,000 feet away.

It was a dark, damp night, and as we drove along the first few miles of straight road the mountains were a black wall in front of us. We went right into it, and from then on there were no more straights. It was an everlasting looping and winding, crossing and recrossing the light railway that has neither level-crossing gates nor fences, headlights swinging past trees and cliffs and pointing out into space over the mountainside with the raindrops falling in the yellow glow, trusting that oncoming traffic would reveal itself by its own headlights before plunging down on to us.

At last we reached Ghoom, the village at the top, and passed a row of shuttered shops with dripping corrugated iron roofs. From then on it was downhill, for Darjeeling lies over the lip of the first range of hills and covers the slopes that face north-west towards the gorge of the Ranjit river and the eternal snows. The plains are hidden away in another world.

We edged up as close to the entrance to the hotel as the big car would go, but it was still not close enough. The pelting rain was like an icy curtain between me and the door. The driver wanted to go home, but I was most unwilling to get out, until eventually, after repeated blasts on the horn, an unhappy watchman, dressed in the khaki tunic of some aged regimental uniform, trotted out with a torch and an umbrella, which gave me a minimal amount of shelter as I transferred my luggage to the porch of the wooden bungalow.

He opened up a bedroom, that was musty with the smell of damp blankets, and showed me a teapot that was still clinging to a last vestige of warmth. On the other side of the bedroom he pointed into a small bathroom built against the sheer rock face, that contained a washbasin and a ewer, a pipe standing out from the rock with a tap on the end of it, and the inevitable thunderbox—the Indian commode. I consoled myself with the thought that, if duty had not sent me, I would never have come.

Next morning things looked rather more cheerful, but even then I could not reconcile myself to my surroundings. Darjeeling, like the other famous hill-stations of the Himalayas—Almora and Mussoorie, Naini Tal and Simla—was acquired by the East India Company from territory ceded by Nepal in 1816 after her defeat in war, and it grew up in the Victorian era, when cold baths, austerity and a minimum of comfort were considered to be good for the soul. In its ramshackle, unsightly buildings with their crude plumbing and primitive heating, it preserves the stamp of a temporary encampment, which might at any time be swept away by a landslide in a particularly heavy monsoon.

Nevertheless, with the growth of the town, the limited land became very valuable, and no doubt the Raja of Sikkim was not unmindful of this fact when his American wife announced in 1966 that the land was his, and that although a small area had been donated to the Company in 1835 by his predecessor, after he had been freed from his position as vassal to the Gurkhas, the rest had been seized illegally in 1850.

That is too long a story to tell here. The fact is that in Darjeeling's first ten years the local people were so impressed by the comparative order and safety of life there that the population rose from 200 to 10,000. It was originally intended as a sanatorium for the Company's servants who had grown ill in the heat of the plains, but very soon it began to fill another role which came to be more important. Several large schools were established there under various Christian religious denominations, and to these the children were sent up from the hot plains as boarders.

If the children could enjoy the cool breezes, there seemed to be no reason why their mothers should not also. So it became customary for the ladies to go "up to the hills" in the "hot weather," and stay in these same primitive boarding houses, with cosy names like Snowview and Windamere [*sic*] and The Snuggery, whilst their husbands bore the heat and burden of the day down below.

Again the wheel turned. With air travel speedy and well-established after the Second World War, most of the Europeans in India stopped sending their children to the local schools and boarded them at home in Europe instead. Either the children would fly out for the summer holidays or the parents would fly home on leave. The schools did not dwindle however. The vacant places were filled up by Indian and other East Asian children whose parents, whether Christian or not, admired the type of disciplined and purposeful education provided there.

One of the best known of these schools is Saint Paul's, which was founded in 1863. The site chosen for it made it probably the highest large secondary school in the world, for it stands at the top of Jalapahar hill, 7,500 feet above sea level.

I set out on foot to visit this school, and after a few minutes' uphill work, I came to the neck of the ridge on which Darjeeling stands. It is called Chowrasta—the Crossroads—and the four roads are the Mall West and the Mall East, which encircle Observatory Hill, the road that leads down into the town, and the road that goes up to Jalapahar. It is thus a kind of central square, where the holidaymakers stroll and the curio shops sell the property of the Tibetan refugees from Cham. A statue of the Nepalese poet, Bhanubhakta, presides over the scene, and the smell of ponies, standing about waiting to be hired, hangs heavy in the air.

I preferred walking to riding, and took the footpath which starts off on the eastern side of the ridge and then crosses over it and joins up with the road. As I climbed, the houses of Darjeeling, scattered amongst the trees and on the open slopes, fell away below, and behind them rose up the great mountains of the Himalaya. Like Lot's wife, I kept turning my head back to look at the unfolding scene. Above everything, fifty miles northwards, at the intersection of the borders of Nepal, Sikkim and Tibet, lay the great snowfields of Kanchenjunga, with the ranges stretching away on either side, and in between stood range upon range of lesser mountains with deep gorges in their folds, through which flowed the turbulant tributaries of the Ranjit and Teesta rivers.

Up at Saint Paul's I found the Rector in his conservatory, with an uninterrupted view of these scenes of grandeur through the glass walls of his office. After thirty years at the school he was now the only European member of the staff left, except for the occasional assistance of a young man doing his Voluntary Service Overseas. He himself was due to retire within a few months, having suffered ill health for some years as a result of injuries sustained in a fall from a horse. But the appointment of a new rector from one of the leading English Public Schools showed that the attempt was being made, within the limitations of Indian staff and Indian pupils, to preserve the alien tradition that had been admired for a hundred years.

Apart from the conservatory, the showpiece of Saint Paul's was the grave of Foss Westcott, Bishop of Calcutta and Metropolitan of India, Burma and Ceylon from 1919 to 1945, who died in 1949. He had been a great character in his time, and I myself had seen him cycling about wartime Calcutta shortly before his retirement, and now he was laid to rest in a mausoleum of unusual magnificence in a setting of unrivalled beauty, surrounded by a circle of lawns of almost imperial splendour, which he himself would have been the last person to expect.

In the afternoon I saw another extract of England, perpetuated with keen attention to ceremony by the independent Indians. A Boy Scouts' investiture was held on the school parade-ground, presided over by the Assistant Area Commissioner, who was himself an old boy of the school. It was, in part, a sad and sentimental occasion, as the opportunity was taken to deliver farewell speeches on the retirement of the Rector. One wondered how long scouting would continue to flourish after he had gone, with the European tea-planters, who were keen supporters, being squeezed out of existence by economic difficulties and the devaluation of the rupee.

I returned to Darjeeling speculating on how long these things would survive, and found it was already time to set out on another visit. The local army commander, who had been expected at the scout investiture, but had been unable to attend because of other duties, was to entertain the Commander-in-Chief, General J. N. Chaudhuri, at the Gymkhana Club, and in India's casually hospitable way I had been invited, as a foreign visitor, to join in.

The path to the club was along the Mall West, skirting round the woods of Observatory Hill. It went past the gate of Government House, the summer residence of Bengal's poetess Governor, Miss Sarojini Naidu, and also past a large sign saying "To the Municipal Latrines", and a large advertisement of the Assam Woodwork Company, promising "flush doors" to would-be purchasers.

Inside the club the wooden dance-hall was full of men and women. Indian Army officers, mostly in tweed and twill suits of European style, mingled with the local aristocracy in their Indian style tunics. Most of the women wore saris, but there was a sprinkling in European dress, the wives of old-time planters, the old *koi hais*, with parchment skins and faded eyes, still lingering on in an alien community.

The bare gallery, supported on grey wooden pillars, loomed emptily above, and a band played ancient dance music as the weak drinks were served. Voices were raised against the creaking wail of the saxophone.

"I say, where are you from, old boy?"

"Look here, old chap, I haven't seen you for ages. Everything *thik hai*?"

"He's a splendid fellow. *Achchha!* I will introduce you to him. Please come with me."

"That was a jolly good show you put up in Poonch, old man. They'd got you in a pretty tight corner there."

"Oh, it's all part of the game, isn't it? The *jawans* were absolutely first class."

"You gave them a pretty good pasting, though."

"Luck. Just luck. I thought I was a goner when I got a shell burst slap in front of me, but my number just was not on it."

"Let's hope it never will be, my dear. What are you drinking? A pint of wallop?"

"Oh, I'm just having a *nimboo pani*. Can't afford beer any more."

"*Achchha!* I'm sticking to Cola."

Sarnath—threshing corn

Benares—by the Burning Ghats

(*above*) Benares—
inside the Monkey
Temple.
(*left*) Darjeeling—the
Tibetan Dancer

"I say, I'm getting down to Calcutta at the end of this month. I want to see a bit of life."

"Much too hot, old man. I'm going on shikar if I can get leave."

"I haven't had a day of leave for two years."

"I say, that's a rotten show, old boy. You must have a jolly tough C.O."

"You know what it's like these days. There's always a flap on. You chaps on the staff don't know what it's like up there."

"Don't you tell me, you old beggar. I've seen plenty of the sharp end."

"*Achchha!*"

"That's the General coming now."

As he spoke the Commander-in-Chief's party came into the centre of the room, and the General, a solid figure of a man, moved amongst the guests, exuding enthusiasm and self-confidence. After a while he led the dancers on to the floor, and then, at a certain moment, the band struck up "For he's a jolly good fellow!" All joined in and followed it up with three cheers.

Shortly afterwards the General left, and the strangely antiquated English talk continued. It seemed symbolic of an army that, because of the financial policy of the Government, was still struggling along on equipment that was more than twenty years old.

General Chaudhuri, who was on a tour of the North-east border regions, had been appointed Commander-in-Chief in 1962 after his predecessor, General Thapar, had resigned as a scapegoat for the débâcle in the face of the Chinese in the same year. His task was to restore the army's morale and provide the equipment to ensure that such a débâcle could not occur again.

The army had felt keenly the humiliation of its defeat and suffered under the attacks of politicians, the majority of whom had never heard a shot fired in anger. Yet, although mistakes undoubtedly were made, a true analysis will show that the Indian Army was placed in as impossible a position as the British Army was in at the time of Dunkirk.

Firstly, ever since independence the Army had suffered under a Defence Minister who, although he had lived in London for many years and had taken an active part in the affairs of the Borough of St Pancras, showed no love for Britain or the West. He therefore could not sympathize with the Indian Army's traditions, which were proudly preserved and maintained from the British days, and

3

placing greater reliance on friendship with the Communist countries of the East, he could not envisage any threat to India's borders apart from the trouble with Pakistan. Money was not forthcoming for the modernization of the army, or even for the building of homes for the soldiers to offset those lost at the time of the partition of India.

Furthermore the Prime Minister, Pandit Nehru, advised by his Defence Minister, Krishna Menon, and brought up on the non-violent principles of Mahatma Gandhi, seemed to feel that to create conditions of peace with his neighbours it was sufficient to speak peace. He heeded not the ancient Indian politics of the Arthashastra, in which it is stated that "the king who is situated anywhere immediately on the circumference of the conqueror's territory is termed the enemy".

Therefore no regrets were officially expressed when China invaded and occupied Tibet in 1950. On the contrary, India voted against the United Nations resolution branding China as an aggressor in Korea and also advocated the admission of China to the United Nations.

From that year onwards the border incidents increased in number. The question was whether to stand firm on the territory within the MacMahon line in the east and the Aksai Chin area in the west, which had been included within the borders of British India, or to accept the premise that the border of the two new republics was subject to negotiation.

Policy vacillated. In 1958 India protested to China over the construction of 100 miles of roadway in the Aksai Chin, but only after the road had been constructed. On the 350-mile eastern sector of the immense 2,000-mile frontier border incidents took place as the Chinese chased rebel Tibetans southwards. These incidents led the Indians to establish frontier posts in the mountain passes, but there were no roads up to these outposts, only pony tracks. Up till 1960 it had been considered safer not to have roads up to the border, but when it became known that the Chinese were building roads on the Tibetan side, the Border Roads Development Board was set up. This was in 1960, and it had not had time to achieve much by 1962.

In fact the only route to the North-east Frontier Agency was through the narrow gap between Nepal and East Pakistan, where the Assam Access road was built in the Second World War, and where later a railway was constructed to skirt round the northern tip of Pakistan and link up West Bengal and Assam.

Having set up the frontier posts, it was inevitable that the army would have to defend them, and this they were called upon to do in no uncertain terms in October 1962. But it was, in fact, the Indians, not the Chinese, who sparked off the actual fighting when Eastern Command was ordered by Delhi to expel the Chinese from the neighbourhood of Dhola near the junction of the borders of India, Tibet and the Indian protected state of Bhutan.

The Chinese were well prepared. They called out at the Indians in Hindi: *"Tum chale jao. Yih zàmin hamari hai. Hindi Chini bhai bhai."* (You go away. This is our land. Indians and Chinese are brothers.) But the Indians were not taken by surprise. At the beginning of October Lieutenant-General Kaul, the second scapegoat of the N.E.F.A. affair, who resigned with General Thapar at the end of November, was appointed commander of a new corps to be formed to meet the Chinese threat.

This corps, however, formed on an *ad hoc* basis, had insufficient manpower to cover such a long frontier, and Army Headquarters was unwilling to reinforce it from the Pakistan frontiers. What was worse, it was equipped with antiquated weapons, insufficient warm clothing for the mountain heights and inadequate digging tools and supply resources. As a consequence the men had to fight ill-armed, exposed and half frozen and starved. As many died of exposure as from the enemy action. Out of a total of 3,250 casualties 1,600 were listed simply as "missing". As for the Air Force, it did not go into action at all, and was confined to a communications role with a few helicopters and light aircraft.

The Chinese attacked in strength on October 20th and threatened Tezpur, the District Headquarters on the Brahmaputra river. The District Commissioner fled, banks closed up and burnt their currency notes and the convicts were released from jail, but the British tea-planters decided to remain. They were vindicated when, on November 21st, the Chinese announced a cease-fire, and on December 1st they commenced to withdraw to a line twenty kilometres behind the line of actual control as it had existed previously.

As a result of this month of disastrous fighting Krishna Menon was, at last, relieved of his duties as Defence Minister, and the defence budget, under the new minister, Chavan, was nearly doubled. In addition small arms were rushed to India by Britain and the U.S.A. with further assistance to the tune of £21 million promised by each country. Ironically enough these arms came in useful in the twenty-two days of fighting, including a tank battle, with Pakistan, which went some way towards retrieving the Indian Army's reputation in 1965.

The day after the party in the Gymkhana Club I went a stage nearer to the border, which plunges down in a spearhead between Sikkim and Bhutan, when I boarded the Land-Rover which takes the mails to Kalimpong every day. My companions included two junior commissioned officers of the Indian Engineers and a silent man from the Mount Everest hotel. We started off at nine o'clock from the bazaar in the lower town, which is nowadays almost entirely populated by Nepalese immigrants, and climbed up to the crossroads at Ghoom before turning left to take the long plunge down to the Teesta river.

In seventeen miles the road drops 7,000 feet, winding its way down through the tea estates, with their own schools and hospitals, to the bridge over the river, which is less than 700 feet above sea-level. Here it crosses the main road to Gangtok, the capital of Sikkim. My passport and special permit were checked by a Bengali police inspector before we were allowed to proceed across the bridge and up the mountain on the other side, and we were again delayed by an army unit which was toiling slowly upwards in a convoy of 3-ton lorries of the kind I knew well in the Second World War. Jumping the queue one by one was tedious and hazardous work, but this was a hot frontier now and I expected to see armed forces everywhere.

The Gurkha officer I had come to see was waiting on the road for me. He took me down to the house he had rented at fifty-five rupees a month for his wife and eight children for the period of his leave, and there he gave me a hot curry lunch. The family served me, but being Brahmins, they would not eat with me and took their food in another room after I had finished. There were two more sons who had already joined up as riflemen and were away with their regiments.

Afterwards we walked out into the town. Before the Chinese occupation of Tibet and the subsequent closing of the frontier it had been full of Tibetans, as it was the first town inside India on the shortest route to Lhasa and known as the listening post of Asia.

But now that the road was barred, this hectic activity had dwindled and Kalimpong had become more of a garrison town for the troops stationed further forward on the trail, which is punctuated by dak bungalows at twelve- to sixteen-mile intervals, where traveller shad been wont to stay the night after the day's stage by pony or on foot.

The place seemed to have settled down to its new role, and the traditional missionary work of the Scottish Universities Mission and Dr Graham's Homes for the children of indigent Anglo-Indians and the Teachers' Training Colleges were carrying on as peacefully as before. The only reminder of the trouble with China, apart from the troops, was the war memorial to three Kalimpong men killed in a Ladakh border incident in 1959.

I would not have been surprised if it had been more than three, for a high proportion of the men who bear the brunt of active service in the Himalayas are Gurkhas and other kindred breeds of India's hillmen. When I pointed this out to my host, he agreed wholeheartedly with me.

In the afternoon I returned to Darjeeling, to the bathroom under the rocky cliff and the thunderbox, and the English boarding-house cooking, which is one of the saddest of the innumerable British legacies to India. But first, before the brown Windsor soup, the tough breast of chicken and two vegetables, drowned in a Sargasso sea of thick sauce, and the cabinet pudding sagging under its bright yellow mantle of custard, we were visited by no less a person than a Maharaja.

Known familiarly to our motherly hostess as Udai and a wealthy landowner, whose property leaped in value with the development of the hill-station, he strolls in from the Planters' club and calls out "Annie!"

"Hallo, Udai!" says Annie.

"What about a drink?"

"O.K., Udai. Take a seat."

The Maharaja sits down with a sigh of satisfaction, hitching up the knees of his tweed suit. He seems to prefer our ramshackle wooden veranda to the marble halls of his own palace. A middle-aged man with grown-up children, he reminisces in the language of the 1920s about the good old days in London, staying at the Carlton, down to the races at Ascot, nights out celebrating, Turkish baths in Jermyn Street to recover. We do not mention the present. It is clearly a matter not to be talked about. Perhaps the present does not even exist, except in some small, faded way, like the pony races on the miniature track down the hill at Lebong. And so the form for the Calcutta Cup tomorrow is discussed with as much intensity as if we were talking about Newmarket or the Derby.

The Maharaja gets up. "Well, old girl," he says to Annie. "I must be getting along."

"O.K., Udai," says Annie. "Come again."

He shakes my hand. "Nice to meet you, my dear fellow," he says. "You come up to my place some time. But things aren't what they were, I'm afraid. We don't have any good parties any more. Can't get the liquor, you see. My God, we had some jolly fine parties during the war, with all the young chaps out from England. Wonderful parties. You ought to have been here then."

"I was," I said.

"Then you know."

"I know."

The Maharaja raised his hand. "Ta ta, Annie!" he said. "I'm off."

He put his tweed hat on his head, took his stick in his hand and walked off up the road towards his palace. I went in to dinner with a group of Scottish banking and business people from Calcutta, who had come "up to the hills" on holiday. The talk was of the difficulties of doing business, the circuitous methods that had to be employed in order to get government licences, the irresponsibility of Indian staff. It seemed a melancholy tale, and one wondered why these people stayed on to wrest a living out of such unfruitful surroundings, but one suspected that, for all its frustrations, life was not so hard and dour as it had been back in Aberdeen and Ayr. This was, after all, the never ending talk of the British business man in India, and possibly the only reason for the increase in frustrations was the greater government control, which restricted free enterprise at every turn.

After listening to an account of all the suffocating controls that they were subject to, I went out for a breath of fresh air. It was about 10.30, but the streets of Darjeeling were already utterly deserted.

Next morning I visited the settlement of the Tibetan refugees, who had fled from the Chinese. Most of them had come into India through Kalimpong as a result of the suppression of the rebellion in the eastern province of Cham.

Bewildered and dazed by the turn of events, they had plodded over the high passes in their big cloth boots, with nothing but the family heirlooms and household goods and a few possessions carried on their backs, and with such of the precious books as they had managed to salvage from the monasteries. India, in spite of her own dire poverty, welcomed them hospitably, set up tented camps for them, and eventually, with the help of foreign aid, opened the Tibetan Refugee School.

The school was on a ledge on the mountainside beneath the northern loop of the Mall. Below it lay Lebong, with its little race-track and military cantonment, and above it towered Kanchenjunga and the line of snows. There was to be a day of religious dances lasting for eight hours, a marathon of endurance from ten in the morning until sunset, and when I arrived the music and dancing were already in full swing.

Large tents, embellished with geometrical designs in squares and circles, surrounded an arena in which figures were twirling like spinning tops. The school-children sat in rows on two sides, on benches and on the ground, whilst the guests were given chairs on the third side.

The bright costumes, the clanging cymbals and thundering gongs, the sharp cries and shouts, and the sudden changes in tempo reminded me immediately of the Chinese folk opera I had seen in Hong Kong and Singapore. But there were many differences. The dancers whirled like dervishes in their big black boots with white upturned toes, whilst the red flaps of their outer jackets and motley bells and network of bobbles flared out horizontal to the ground. As well as enormous headdresses there were weird black masks, looking like a cross between a primitive Hindu idol and a Melanesian totem, and white masks and long cloth noses. The chorus was a series of long drawn-out melancholy and melodious cries, evocative of the barren heights in which these mountain people live. The speech was in a formalized, gabbled monotone.

The king in his high crown, the queen with her great emerald halo, the minister in his big golden headgear like the state turban of a Persian wazir, the men in trilby hats holding a blue cloth up to their waists to represent a ship at sea—all had their parts to play. There were stags and deer and leopards, and comic interludes suddenly changing to the mystical, like the medieval mystery plays, but the marathon part was the role of the boy, danced by a youngster who looked to be scarcely in his teens, with a seraphic smile of artistic absorption on his face.

And this was scarcely surprising, for in the long and complicated fairy story the boy is the hero. A strange mixture of folk tale and religion, the Padma Wobar tells how Buddhism was brought to Ceylon, but the Indian names and places are quite unrecognizable in their Tibetan version. In the English version, printed by the Freedom Press, we are told how, once upon a time there was a kingdom in India called Muteg-ched, with its capital, Namkha Muna, ruled over by King Lokpechoje, who was not a Buddhist. He had great confidence in one of his ministers, named Kangjong Bang Chen.

Amongst the king's other ministers there was a man named Tschangpon Norsang, who was a devout Buddhist, and the king was afraid he might become too powerful and change the official religion of his kingdom. So, in order to get rid of him, he ordered him to set out over the sea in search of some precious jewels in a far off land. His ship was destroyed by two strangers, and he died at sea.

Meanwhile his wife, who was an incarnation of a goddess, gave birth to a son. When the boy grew up, he wanted to know who his father was, but his mother refused to tell him. So, after some years, he took some of his mother's wool, twisted it into yarn and took it to the market-place, where he found an old woman. The boy and the old woman exchanged their threads of yarn, but soon the old woman was lamenting that she had finished up the boy's yarn and he had taken away her life. The boy promised to return her own yarn to her if she would tell him who his father was.

The king had been watching this scene through binoculars, and after calling in the old woman for questioning, he got the truth out of her. Greatly perturbed, he ordered the boy to set out over the sea in search of some precious jewels in a far off land.

His mother went to the pagoda to pray, and she was told that, if the boy repeated the holy formula of Buddhism—Buddha, Dharma and Sangha—all would be well. When the two strangers appeared, who had destroyed his father's ship, he repeated the formula and they disappeared. Eventually he reached the Island of Golden Sands and the palace of Naga. He found the jewels and returned home, but when he got back, the king upbraided him for being so long about it and sent him off to Ceylon to bring back the mystical

Golden Gong. When he reached Ceylon, the queen who ruled there allowed him to take the Golden Gong, and not only that. He brought back with him a group of women too, on whom he had conferred the blessing of the Buddha.

When the king saw the group of women as well as the gong, he told the boy he had committed a great crime and would be executed. Thereupon the executioner was summoned and a great fire lit. The boy was burnt to death, and the women of Ceylon collected his bones and ashes, from which a lily grew. Guru Padma Sambhava appeared out of the lily, and the women of Ceylon then asked the king to fly round the world on the magic Golden Gong. He and his minister were then taken up into the sky on the Golden Gong and thrown over Ceylon, where they were both eaten by the people. From that day on Guru Padma Sambhava was King of Ceylon. It became a Buddhist country and the people became very happy.

I stayed for no more than two hours of this whirling, fantastic story, which must have been told a thousand times at the monastery festivals in high Tibet, but had never before been seen in India. Then I went back to the boarding house by way of the hill which is said to have been the first inhabited part of Darjeeling.

The summit is called Mahakal, in honour of the god, Siva, whose cave is to be found there. This is clearly Hindu, although the Buddhists still cling to the spot with their prayer flags and the chorten containing the relics of the holy man, Dorje Lama. The first thing I came to was a hideous temple built in 1958 to house an image of Kali, Siva's fearsome consort. It had been built by the West Bengal Tribal Area Aid Organization, and one wondered in what conceivable way this monstrous building could aid the tribes.

A rheumy-eyed Buddhist from Gangtok came forward, explaining to me how all religions are one, and insisted on giving me a rose and a yellow calico prayer flag overprinted with the scriptures. Then the Hindu approached, an insolent Brahmin from Katmandu, in order to ensure that a suitable temple offering was made.

I retreated from this attack up the steps to the platform from which the place derives its modern name of Observatory Hill. The platform was bare, the telescope having been removed, and a pleasant place was thus left abandoned to the dirt and offal of backward-looking superstition.

My brief stay in the Hills was near its end, but there was one more visit I had to make before taking the road down to the plains again. It was to the most famous and oldest established of all the schools in Darjeeling—the Loreto convent, founded in 1846.

Since that date the convent has gone from strength to strength, with a large vernacular day school added to the secondary boarding establishment. As in the fraternal Jesuit School, Saint Joseph's College, at North Point, nearly all the pupils are now Indian or East Asian, their parents accepting the religion for the sake of the education.

I was received with a certain special interest because of my name, which was linked with Forbesgunj, the nondescript railway station I had passed through in Bihar. For Forbes of Forbesgunj, who died less than twenty years ago, sent his daughters to the convent, and having made money planting indigo, he built the large assembly hall, which is named after him, proving that even a Scotsman can be catholic in his benevolence.

I was shown this impressive hall, which is large enough for indoor games as well as school functions, and was pleased to think that a member of the clan had been responsible for its construction. Then I met Mother Antoinette, aged eighty-five, and the oldest member of the staff. Like the Maharaja she reminisced nostalgically about the gay wartime parties, and rambled on about the girls of the Women's Royal Army Corps of India, who had been billeted in Forbes Hall, and the U.S. servicemen who had come to visit them, dishing out pockets full of candy to adults as well as to children.

The same evening the Roman Catholic hierarchy, led by the Bishop in his red skullcap, turned out in force to attend the school concert. Demure schoolgirls, dressed in white, sang and played the piano, and a costume piece, called the Domes of Isfahan, brought the entertainment to an end on a colourful note. I thought that, though this was taking place in the far north-eastern corner of India on the border of Tibet, it might have been anywhere from San Francisco to Singapore.

Next day I left Darjeeling, thinking of all the mixture of races and religions thrown together in a small place that was once merely a sanatorium for people who were overheated and ill. Bengalis and other Indians, Nepalis, Tibetans and British; Buddhists, Hindus and Christians of many sects; they are all there, and many others, each group distinctive and separate, for India accepts everything but assimilates nothing. She simply adds the new to the old as yet another item in the infinite variety of human existence.

In many ways Darjeeling had stood still. People looked back at the wartime years as at a kind of high point of excitement, which had simply been followed by decline. And I too looked back. I thought of the trek I had made through the rhododendron forests of Sandakphu and up to the bare heights of Phallut on the Singalela Range, and into Sikkim to visit the Monastery of Pamionchi. In those days the hike into the folds of the Himalayas, with three stalwart, laughing Bhotiya women to carry the camp kit, had seemed like an excursion into the peace of another world. It was clear, now, that this peace had been indefinitely shattered, and the whole region sucked into the stress and strife of modern politics and the struggle of existence.

3

THE BLACK PAGODA

I WENT back to the plains in a battered car with a Nescafé salesman and a slim Sikh as fellow-passengers. There was heavy rain, and a tree had fallen across the road, which we circumvented with difficulty. Half-way down, near Kurseong, the car developed the inevitable mechanical defect. It was trouble with the petrol, although we had been dangerously freewheeling most of the way in order to conserve fuel.

In fact the usual muddle and confusion of travel in India soon developed. At Siliguri station no one could tell me whether the berth I had tried to reserve by telephone from Darjeeling had, in fact, been allotted to me. The only way to make certain was to go ten miles in the wrong direction to New Jalpaiguri station, which had been constructed after the existing Jalpaiguri had become a dead end up against the frontier of East Pakistan. Here, where the platforms had been built but the station offices were still in bamboo bashas, it was necessary to find the chief ticket collector and discuss at length the simple question as to whether or not my name had been, was being or might be attached to a berth on the night train.

Eventually the decision was made in the affirmative, and the train started off. First it went back to Siliguri, and then through the night down to the Ganges, which we reached early next morning. There I got mixed up with a jostling crowd of porters, one of whom ran off with my kit on the top of his head. This was followed by an hour on the steamer, for the bridge, too, was now in East Pakistan, and the new bridge over the Ganges further upstream was not yet completed.

Then it was necessary to climb into another train on the south bank of the river and sit shaken and jostled till evening time, when it finally dragged itself into swarming, stifling Sealdah station in Calcutta. I was driven out from Sealdah to Barrackpore, where troops are still stationed after nearly 200 years. We cut across the corner of an airfield, and there was a roaring of aircraft engines coming through the hot, still night.

It all smelt strangely familiar, for this was one of the airfields I had helped to lay out during the Second World War. I remembered the trouble we had had filling in the water tanks that lay across the path of the runway, and the diesel road-rollers sinking up to their axles in the spongy surface which developed because the water had not been properly pumped out. In those days it had served the Assam and Burma fronts. Now it was in the front line facing Pakistan not fifty miles away.

With the drone of the aero-engines still in my ears I settled my kit in one of the rooms in the small transit camp for the British Brigade of Gurkhas, which still remained in Barrackpore. Then one of the officers took me down to spend an hour or so at the club.

Barrackpore Club, as I remembered it, had been full of life and activity, jam-packed in the evenings with those enjoying the "gay" wartime life, which the Maharaja and Mother Antoinette had recalled. Now there was nobody. Passing through the Corinthian columns of the entrance one came upon an empty hall, where scarcely a thing had been removed except for the people that had given it life. Sketches by Boz still hung over the bar, one still bought one's book of chits for drinks, and the same pile of magazines still stood in the corner, though the Overseas *Daily Mirror* had joined since my time and the *Tatler* had resigned.

It did not matter, for there was nobody to read them, and even if there had been, the electric light was too dim to read by. The swimming pool was empty, but it was unthinkable to wade out into the muddy Hooghly, that swept past the bottom of the sun-dried lawn. So one just sat and chatted and gazed across at the dim outline of the opposite bank, and watched with patient interest the slow approach of a country sailing boat, labouring its way up this waterway, which in the Company's time had been the main means of communication with the hinterland of Upper India.

And on that opposite bank lay Chandernagore, which the French held for nearly 300 years until 1951, and Chinsura, which the Dutch clung to for 180 years until they swopped it for the huge island of Sumatra, and one may imagine got the best of the bargain, even though they had to pay £100,000 in cash as well.

All drowned now in the dust bath of the Indian Republic, the history of these places survives in little churches with locked doors and battered shutters, in graveyards and memorial tablets which are meaningless to the thousands who mill around them, and in memories preserved in books in European libraries. What Indian king, sitting in the great courts of Delhi or Hyderabad or Bijapur, could ever have imagined that out of these little groups of irascible *feringhees,* fighting and squabbling, attacking without declaring war, as Clive did against the Dutch at Biderra in 1759, making allies of native princes against each other, then dropping them or defeating them in their turn as soon as their usefulness was past, would emerge one group that would rule them all.

A couple of days later I left Calcutta again to visit the remains of a people who grew to prominence long before the *feringhees* came to India, and left monuments which they never equalled. The train was the Puri express, and I shared my compartment with a group of Bengalis who were going to the seaside for a holiday. Early next morning we were running through the peaceful countryside of Orissa, crossing sandy rivers where the people were washing themselves and excreting in the cool light, which was already strong enough to give warning of the blazing day to come.

Across the plain great blocks of trellis work stood on banked-up ramparts like primitive walled towns. They were the vineyards of the pan leaf, exported mostly to Calcutta and Benares, which the Bengali chews indefatigably with his betel nut and then spits out on to the floor or pavement. The pan vines are tended by the Oriya women, whom I could see on the village paths with their white metal armlets, anklets and bracelets setting off their skins of polished dark mahogany. They looked well fed this year, though once before I had seen them parched and wrinkled with famine. But it was always the same in India. There was never enough stored from the fat years to carry them over the lean.

I got out of the train at Bhubaneshwar, leaving the holiday-makers to carry on to the sea, and found a pedal rickshaw to take me to the tourist bungalow. It was brand new, and so was the whole of the city, for this was the new capital of Orissa, with its own air-field, government offices, hospital, universities, schools, Hindu temple, Buddhist vihara, Christian church and Moslem mosque. There was even a state guest-house and a tribal research bureau, with additional large areas set aside for a military cantonment, an agricultural farm, a "regional poultry farm", and a hydraulic research station.

As set out in the plan by Solomon S. Reuben, the Government Architect, and P. C. Das, the Additional Chief Engineer, it looked magnificent. But for the moment I had no time for more than a brief glimpse at the broad avenues and the cream-coloured rectangular official buildings lying well back from them, into which the breath of life had scarcely entered. After Calcutta it was a blessed relief to see a city with hardly any people in it, yet doubtless the teeming crowds would soon begin their invasion and there would soon be ten or twenty people somehow living off each productive working individual.

In many of the key centres of attraction in India the tourist bungalows have now taken the place of the dak bungalows, which were originally staging posts on the routes the mail took, or the Circuit houses, Public Works Department inspection bungalows and government rest-houses, for accommodation in which the guide book counselled application in advance, or those Indian versions of station hotels, called the railway retiring rooms, in which one unrolled one's bedding and slept after walking down the platform to the upper-class restaurant for one's dinner. They are show places, tastefully decorated, with bronze figures of Siva dancing in his circle of flame on the prostrate body of the wicked Asura, and colourful pamphlets and magazines on low tables beside reclining chairs covered in bright chintzes. And if the lock on the lavatory door is on the outside instead of the inside and there is trouble with the water cistern, one has to remember that the plumbing problem, which the British did not seem able to solve in a hundred years, cannot be overcome in a fifth of that time.

I left this protective oasis a few minutes after I arrived, and plunged into the sweat and dust of India again in order to catch a bus for the Black Pagoda of Konarak. It was a moment of tightening emotion, for here was I taking my seat and paying my rupee for a bus ticket in a public conveyance that was going to take me to one of those places that haunt the imagination for ever until one actually sees them face to face. I had just the same feeling as I experienced boarding a bus in Athens with the destination sign "Thebes" above the driver's cab, and catching one in Jerusalem bound for Bethlehem.

But nothing could be more different from both these places than Konarak. It was forty miles across the plain, with a halt at a poor looking village called Pipli, where people got out to buy mangoes. There was a rash of roadside signs such as, "Excess Population

Upset Country's Plan", and "National Malaria Eradication Programme—World's Greatest". They were all in English, and few people out of the vast masses they were aimed at would be able to read them. But they were like talismans, as if the signs themselves would help in some magical way, like tantric formulae, to achieve the desired result.

At Nimpada an old stone plinth, with two surviving arches and fragments of elaborate carving on it, gave a sign of the former civilization of the region in a squalid village that had reverted from the stone to the bamboo and mud and wattle age. Our appetite was then progressively whetted by more road signs. At fifteen miles distance the sign read, "Temple of Konarak, where dream is realized in stones"; at ten miles, "Famous Black Pagoda of Konarak"; at five miles, "Look forward for a view of Konarak Temple (You can see it across the plain as mariners from the sea)".

It was true. Above an avenue of young casuarina trees the top of the great pile of stone could just be seen, blackened by the sea air and the sun. This was what the seamen, coasting from Madras to Calcutta, saw across the intervening two miles of sandy littoral which has built up during the centuries since the temple was built, and this is what gave it its English name. As well as an air of fantastic mystery, it had a sinister reputation, for there were large wrought iron beams built into it, which acted on the ships' compasses and set them awry.

One thinks of the Black Pagoda as belonging to some ancient, far-off pagan order of things, which has been long dead, but in fact, like nearly all the famous stone temples of India, it is of far more recent origin than the great ruins of the Persian and Roman worlds that survive in the Near East. These temples are medieval in our way of reckoning—the Indian counterpart, if you like, of the soaring cathedrals of the western world.

The temple at Konarak is said to have been built in the thirteenth century, when Orissa had been the centre of the Lion dynasty of the Kesaris for over 700 years. If so, it is far more recent than the temples at Bhubaneshwar, which was the capital of the kingdom until Nripati Kesari moved it to Cuttack in the tenth century, and more modern, too, than the White Pagoda at Puri.

The atmosphere of great antiquity which it exudes is therefore false. Even if the main structure were to have been built in the ninth century—and I am inclined to join the minority who believe

Bhubaneshwar—the sacred pool

Konarak—a wheel of the Sun Chariot

in the earlier date—it would still be no older than the rest of the profusion of temple buildings in this small part of Orissa, except for the high towers of the White Pagoda at Puri and the Great Pagoda of Bhubaneshwar.

Yet the other two live, whilst this one has died and fallen into decay. Sucking in twelve years' revenue from a fertile land, and the offerings, no doubt, of countless pilgrims, it seems to have grown up in an orgasm of building, and then collapsed into the most orgiastic ruins in the world.

Some say the tower was never completed. Others affirm that it was finished and was over 220 feet high, two thirds the height of St Paul's Cathedral, but fell down later. Either the sandy foundations were unable to support the great weight of the stone superstructure, or else it was struck by lightning—a likely probability in view of the iron it contained.

The latter have the testimony of Abu'l Fazl, who wrote at the end of the sixteenth century and said that it was 150 cubits high. Certain it is that part of the tower was still standing in 1837, for Fergusson, the great pioneer student of Indian architecture, saw it there, though he missed the significance of the iron beams. Certain it is, also, that the temple was "live" for hundreds of years, since ancient palm-leaf records at Puri state that there were twelve great annual festivals, the most important of which was celebrated in the month of Magh (January/February). Kings made large endowments for the expenses, and vast numbers of pilgrims crowded into the temple and on to the seashore to witness them, just as they do to this day at the White Pagoda.

The death of the Black Pagoda was, in fact, as extraordinary as its growth, which was based on a story of the god Krishna. According to the legend Samba, one of Krishna's sons, once incurred the anger of a holy man, who bore false witness against him in order to avenge himself. He lured Samba to a lake, where Krishna's wives were bathing, and then told Krishna that he was trying to seduce them. Krishna impetuously cursed Samba with leprosy.

Eventually Krishna learned the truth, and told Samba, who had become a wandering outcast leper, that his only hope of a cure lay with Surya, the Sun God. After twelve long years he was rewarded with a vision of the god on a lotus leaf, and at this spot the temple was built.

According to the Brahmins at Puri worship continued at Konarak

4

until the sixteenth century. The Black Pagoda then lost its magnetic power and became a "dead" temple. And in this case the power actually was magnetic, for the divine fluence of the shrine was literally contained in a loadstone. The Puri Brahmins say the magnet was stolen by a renegade Hindu. Others make Mohammedan sailors responsible, who were wrecked on the shore by its effect on their navigation.

One first sees the full size of the pagoda when one walks up to the lip of the large rectangular basin in which it now stands, cleared of the debris of ages. It appears to be below the surface of the ground, but this is because the level of the land around it has risen up to the top of the surrounding wall. The buildings, even without the central tower, still rise high above the land round about, and people clambering over the ruins look like pygmies.

After a few seconds to focus the eyes one can see some of the twenty-four wheels, twice the height of a man, on which the huge building is supposed to ride. At the far end seven horses with seven horsemen pull it towards the East, towards the rising sun, for this is the chariot of Surya, the sun god.

It thus has an apocalyptic significance, the seven horses representing the seven days of the week, twenty-four wheels to tally with the twelve months, each divided into the light and dark of the Hindu almanac, eight spokes to each wheel for the eight divisions of the day. For this is the eastern edge of the land of the Hindus, the opposite of Somnath on the western edge, where the image of the god was said to be suspended in air within a loadstone canopy.

The sack of Somnath by Mahmud of Ghazni and the looting of the temple of the setting sun has been related by a historian from Qazvin in Persia, but no one has detailed the demise of the temple of the rising sun at Konarak. Yet the sun gods still stand there on the northern, southern and western sides, regal and imperishable in the hard, imported stone, epitomizing, no doubt, the king himself, with diminutive figures at his feet adoring him. In front of one of them stands a sacrificial altar with a frieze of elephants below and human worshippers above.

These are not the figures that attract the attention, however, for the picture at Konarak is one of movement, not rigidity. The lions dragging the elephants to the ground, symbolic of the traditional Kesari conquest of Buddhist Magadha, the big free standing statues in the courtyard of the elephant with a warrior in its trunk and the warhorse trampling on a primitive man with crisped hair and a curved kukri for a weapon, the horses straining on the ropes of the great chariot itself, all conjure up a picture of stress and drama and passion. So, too, do the hundreds of carvings, filling every vacant space on the huge structure, to which the eyes inevitably are drawn, for they represent the passion of sex in all the postures that can be conceived.

These sex carvings, though natural to the Hindu, have exercised the minds of westerners ever since they first saw them. Laurence Hope put the query in the Reverie of Mahomed Akram:

An elephant hunt, a musicians' feast—
And curious matings of man and beast;
What did they mean to the men who are long since dust?
   Whose fingers traced,
   In this arid waste,
These rioting, twisted figures of love and lust?

Strange, weird things that no man may say,
Things Humanity hides away;—
   Secretly done,—
Catch the light of the living day,
   Smile in the sun.

She called her poems the Garden of Kama, and Kama is the Hindu god of love, so perhaps love is a good thing to bear in mind, for so much nonsense has been written about the meaning of these copulating couples on the temple walls that it is easy to forget what they actually portray.

In modern times the strange fancy has grown up that all these men and women, carved with loving care in a hundred different amorous poses, ranging from the tender embrace to the basic act of coition, have been put there to protect the building from lightning or the evil eye. The odd idea that obscene carvings would scare away wicked spirits was voiced by E. B. Havell, the former keeper of the Calcutta art gallery. One would have thought a vicious mind would be more likely to be attracted than repelled.

The opposite theory of attraction rather than repulsion would have it that the people liked to look at them, and were therefore attracted by them to the temples. This is a plausible idea if one imbues the simple Indian peasant with the mind of the modern westerner with his insatiable interest in viewing sexual activity from the outside. It is improbable for two reasons. Firstly it is typical of the erotic carvings on Indian temples to be on the outer walls. In very few are there any inside, and those which are inside are usually small and difficult to see and unattractive. Therefore, if this theory were valid, the pilgrims would stay outside instead of going inside. Secondly, a little quiet observation of pilgrims at these temples shows that they pay little attention to the embellishments, having come to partake of the power of the goddess or god and not to study pornographic art.

The fact that the erotic carvings are nearly all on the outside walls of the temples has led to the third theory—that pilgrims are meant to satiate themselves with the contemplation of carnality and sexuality outside, so that when they enter the sanctuary of the god, they will be cleansed and freed of all such thoughts. This theory was put forward by Yeats-Brown in his best-seller, *The Lives of a Bengal Lancer*. But I find it hard to believe that the Temple Superintendent at Puri ever said to him the words he puts into his mouth, for since the god himself is the epitome and acme of sexuality, usually represented by a sexual organ in stone, to make men put sex right out of their minds before entering his presence would seem to be absurd.

These theories have been put forward by westerners, who appear to have little concept of the Hindu mind. We come closer to the truth when we listen to what the Indians, themselves, have to say. According to A. K. Coomaraswamy the figures in coitus, known as *maithunas*, appear on the temple walls simply because voluptuous ecstasy has its due place in life, and those who interpreted life were artists. This is plausible up to a point, but it does not explain why these figures almost cover the walls of some temples, whilst on others they are scarcely to be seen. Mulk Raj Anand, in his study of the subject in *Kama Kala*, gets closer to grips with the reality when he refers to oneness in God, and the fact that the union of the male and the female is the intensest joy in nature, and represents in nature the cosmic union of the symbolic male and female organs— the *lingam* and the *yoni*—which are worshipped in the shrine.

The truth is that the erotic temple carvings of India have become very much more widely known and discussed in this generation than in the last. The *Kama Kala*, mentioned above, the *Kama Kalpa*, and the *Kama Shilpa*, lavishly illustrated, have made it possible for a number of people to see what they are like without the trouble and expense of going to India themselves. They can simply buy the books, though one publisher expects them to declare that they are members of the medical or legal professions, scholars, or research students of Indology, psychology or the social sciences. Furthermore, the two prime examples of temples with a profusion of erotic carvings on them—at Konarak and at Khajuraho—have been made the principal goals of our latter-day pilgrims, the tourists.

Wandering round the great entrance hall, called the Jagmohan, which is the largest part of the temple of the sun that remains, and along the wall of the remaining part of the inner sanctuary from which the tower has fallen, and gazing at those curving, embracing figures, carved in the soft laterite and hardened in the sun, I made my own assessment of their meaning and *raison d'être*.

With careful consideration it is possible to see a clear history of the carvings of male and female couples on the walls of Indian temples. In the far-off Buddhist days, as represented at Sanchi and Ajanta and other places, the couples are simple and demure—a man and woman standing side by side, or perhaps holding hands and looking at each other. They seem to represent the ordinary love of a common man for his faithful spouse.

In later generations, with the influence of the dark Dravidian imagination of the south, the simple Buddhism of Asoka withers away. The Buddha becomes absorbed into the vast and varied paganism that westerners came to call Hinduism, and remains simply as the ninth incarnation of Vishnu, and not the most important one either.

And what becomes of the simple couples at the door? To put it simply, restraint and modesty disappear. They are no longer in the presence of the great renunciation, of the teacher who turns his back on the passions of the world; they are in the courts of the great dancer, of Siva Nataraja—Lord of Dance—of the fertility god of the Tamil South, who is worshipped in the form of the erect phallus.

To honour the dancing god the Nath Mandir, the dance hall, is set up. It still survives at Konarak, facing the main door, with a frieze of dancers and female musicians playing the flute and drum. The Devadasis, devoted to the service of the god, perform the ritual dances at festival time. The god is no longer superhuman, turning his back on the pleasures and miseries of the world. The common people, who throng the temples, conceive of him as simply more than human, with primal appetites for reproduction and destruction, for sex and slaughter, that are cosmic in magnitude.

The god is given a mate, who clings to him in a tight-knit embrace, both creating and absorbing the strength of his body. And it is this *shakti*, this power of the god, that men adore, gaining his power through her. As Christians, not daring to approach the deity direct, seek him through the mediation of the Virgin Mary, so the Siva *bhakti*, the devotees of Siva, approach him through his *shakti*.

The generations pass, and nothing stands still. The devotion becomes warmer, the dance more like a Bacchic frenzy, the Deva-dasis become the temple prostitutes for the male devotees to enjoy. According to the Abbé Dubois, who lived at Seringapatam in the early nineteenth century, they were originally reserved exclusively for the Brahmins, but in the latter days sold themselves to all comers. One imagines that there was no more romance about them than about the women of Grant Road, Bombay, whose price is about the equivalent of three shillings.

But the sexual act with the Devadasis is not mere physical enjoyment. It is a mystical act of union with the *shakti*, and a part of the increasingly involved magical and astrological ritual necessary to approach the deity and tap his power. The place of the *maithunas*, the carvings of sexual congress, on the walls of the temples now becomes clear. Bhubaneshwar is described in the Government of India pamphlet as "the cathedral city of India", and as in the cathedrals, the carvings, statues and paintings of the temple are picture galleries for the illiterate to tell the religious story to the simple peasants, who can neither read nor write.

The *maithunas* show the pilgrims the many different forms the sexual act of union might take. In the manner of the pin-ups outside strip shows in modern cities, far from calming the appetites they serve to whet them, like an aphrodisiac, in honour of the great reproducer. Some, indeed, are so advanced as to be anatomically impossible except for contortionists.

This interpretation may sound crude, and not very nice to the modern admirers of Hindu art and culture. In their contemplation of the art of the dead figures, which are so vivid that they almost seem to leap out at you from the hot, grey stone, they forget the heat and sweat and stark primary colours of the living temple, the pandars taking fees like brothel-keepers for a few minutes of sex with a temple girl, the dirt and disease and lack of any sanitation.

Yet there is ample written testimony that the late medieval Hindu ritual included the sexual unions of men and women, of which the stone picture gallery on the walls is simply a natural illustration, with the same attention to detail in stone as the Kamasutra pays to detail in words.

Nowadays the frenzy and orgy of the temples, which was still in its late flowering when the first Europeans entered on the scene, has died down. It is the western visitor who is agog, whom the guide seizes to point out to him, lest he should miss them, the most lubricious of the effigies that he can find. The Indian just laughs. He has seen it all before. And if man and woman, why not man and beast? For beasts, to him, are not soulless as they are to the Christian divines. Though different in shape and without the gift of speech, they are of the same living essence. They have their humanity too.

As I walked away from the sight of these things on the walls of the Black Pagoda, I wondered what manner of a man it was who had conceived such a construction. And later, after I had left India, I saw him. Standing in one of the cool corridors of the Victoria and Albert Museum in London, with the groups of children walking past, munching chocolate and sweets, I gazed upon the god king, who was the creator of this massive hymn to fertility and the centre of the web in which it stood.

I was looking at a small piece of stone with a group of figures carved on it. King Narasinha Deva, the "Lion God," was sitting cross-legged before a priest, who held a fly-whisk in his hand. He wore nothing but a loin-cloth and was attended by two youths, similarly clad, with four warriors below. He had ear-lobes elongated like those on the Easter Island statues, and long, thin, waxed moustachios, and on his face he wore a satisfied smile.

The sun beat down on the ruins of its temple with increasing heat as I left it behind me. I stopped under a casuarina tree and a local villager sliced the top off a coconut for me to drink the milk. But no longer is it true that "no supplies can be got at Konarak except milk and perhaps eggs, and the traveller will do well to take even his drinking water with him". A hundred yards down the road the new tourist bungalow beckons one into its cool interior, and one is back amongst the bright chintzes and the low tables, leaving the "rioting, twisted figures of love and lust" baking in the mid-day heat.

After the Black Pagoda the temples of the old town—the

"cathedral" town—of Bhubaneshwar were something of an anti-climax. But at least it was possible to see what the great tower of the Sun temple must have looked like before it collapsed. The *deul*, or tower, of the Lingaraja temple rises 127 feet above the ground. It is cigar-shaped, composed of tier upon tier of stone ribs, which are flat or semi-circular. The ribs curve inwards at the top to form a flattened surface, on which sit eight huge lions that support a circular ribbed cap, called the *amalaka*. Perched on this stands the *kalasa*, an egg-shaped pinnacle crowning everything except the flag of Vishnu, which flies over all.

It was the following morning when I approached this temple, but I was not allowed to enter, although Rupees 73,423 of government money had been spent on its restoration in 1925, when Sir Henry Wheeler, KCSI, KCIE, was Governor of Bihar and Orissa. However, there were no restrictions on visiting the smaller shrines, which stood dotted about the place like enormous beehives. From some of them the honey was gone, and they had become ancient monuments. Others were still guarded by priests, who demanded the removal of shoes, even though I had taken care not to wear leather ones, and the payment of fees.

At one beehive, beside a tank where women were bathing, there was a charming archway, decorated with reclining female figures, which was called a *torana* and looked like the authentic prototype of the Japanese *tori*. On another many of the carvings had been wantonly disfigured, with faces and sexual organs sliced off, clearly by some puritanical enemy. In the tank of the Kedareshwar temple people were not only bathing but also drinking the same water. An old man told me that there was iron in it and it was a good cure for dyspepsia. I could not help thinking that they did things differently in Harrogate and Bath.

Some of the beehives were in ruins. Others had saplings sprouting out of them, forcing the stonework into distorted shapes like the Hindu ruins the jungle has taken over in Cambodia. Others had scaffolding on them and were being restored. I hoped the restoration would not go so far as plastering them with whitewash and painting the figures pink and blue, for the bare, warm stone seemed to be the right colour for these relics of the past in their last long sleep. In one, standing on its own on a low mound across the paddy fields, I found a stone bull, decorated with petals—Nandi, the sacred vehicle of Siva. Workmen were sleeping beside it in the cool shade of the interior. Outside, the sun blazed down on the round-hipped, big-breasted dancers petrified in the poses of today's "art" magazines.

Next day I followed the holidaymakers down to the sea at Puri. Like Konarak it was a name to conjure with, for the White Pagoda at Puri is the home of Jagannath, and the first Europeans to visit the place called his huge chariot the Juggernaut, thus coining a new word for the English language.

The Sanskrit meaning of Jagannath is the same as Bhubaneshwar. He is Lord of the World, and the great tower of his temple rises to 190 feet, almost the same height as the Black Pagoda must have been. Though tradition has it that there has been a temple on this spot to house the sacred image since the fourth century, the present building was put up in the twelfth century by a Kesari king in expiation of the offence of killing a Brahmin.

It has prospered ever since. In the eighteenth and nineteenth centuries donations poured into its treasuries from the Bengali devotees of Vishnu. It underwent major renovations just after the First World War, and was again redecorated after India had gained her independence to become a dazzling white landmark across the Orissan plain. The carved figures on the tower were painted up in gold, whilst the garments of the lesser figures below were coloured in the primary peasant colours of blue, red and green, and the flesh tinted a shade of ochre more Chinese than Indian. So important is it to the Hindu world today that Jagadguru Shankaracharya, the High Priest of Puri, is frequently referred to as the Pope of Hinduism and the weight of his injunctions against the slaughter of cows is felt heavily in distant Delhi, especially when combined with a two months' fast.

As I rode in a pedicab towards the town, I could see the white tower in front of me. It was the same shape as the beehives of Bhubaneshwar, with the wheel of Vishnu above the topmost pinnacle and the god's red flag flying on a tall flagpole above everything. I was now approaching a "live" temple that gave me some idea of what the Black Pagoda must have looked like before it died.

Of its living activity there was no doubt, for the great doorway, guarded by two grinning white lions, was thronged with people going in and out, dressed mostly in the simple white cloth of the pilgrim. As I approached, an old, bald man emerged, bare to the waist, with a white *dhoti* round his lower limbs and the Brahminical thread looped from his right shoulder down to the left side of his waist, who looked like a living Gandhi.

As if they had been lying in wait for me or appointed specially to prevent some impious act, two men leaped forward to bar my entry. One of them had a further motive, which was to conduct me, for a consideration, to the upper storey of a house lying close to the side wall of the temple precincts, so that, like some small boy being given a treat, I could peep over and get a better view.

In fact the view was not much better than the one at the doorway, though it was possible to see more easily the layout of the sacred enclosure, with its Hall of Offerings, its dance hall, its Hall of Audience, where the faithful wait to take their turns in viewing the idol, and the sanctuary beneath the high tower, which is the actual residence of the god.

I was disappointed. "Why can't I go inside?" I said to the smooth young man.

"Only Hindus allowed," he said.

"You haven't asked me whether I am a Hindu," I said.

"Only Hindus. You no Hindu."

"How do you know I'm not a Hindu? You say that just because I've got a white face."

"Ah. You know! We Indians are Hindus."

"Have I got to have a black or brown face to be a Hindu? Can I become a Hindu?"

"You cannot be a Hindu."

"No? Well, I'm not a Hindu. But tell me what does your great god look like? What does the Hindu god look like, that all those people have come to see?"

"Cannot say."

"Surely, you can say. You must have seen him many times. Have you seen him?"

"Yes, I have seen him."

"What does he look like, then?"

"Cannot say. He is different things to different people."

"Tell me what he looks like to you."

"I do not understand."

We left the upper storey, and I returned to the great door. From it a broad road, partly asphalted, stretches dead straight for a mile to another, smaller temple. It is the road the huge wooden chariot takes during the annual car festival. For the time being, however, half its width was taken up by small traders, selling religious amulets and pictures, children's toys and all kinds of knick-knacks, at open air booths, and I soon discovered it was very easy to see what the idol of the Lord of the World looks like. I bought a shiny colour print, divided into four parts, called Sri Jagannath No 2 and done by one, J. P. Sharma, with the serial number 1068 in the Roman script overprinted on it.

I saw that on each of the four parts there were three faces—white, black and yellow. The white one, on the left, represented the Lord of the World, worshipped as Krishna, the eighth incarnation of Vishnu; the black one, on the right, was his brother, Balbhadra, and the yellow, smaller one, between them, was his sister, Subhadra.

But one could really hardly call them faces. They were grotesque masks, caricatures of faces with the features outlined in red or yellow and framed in circles or half ellipses of the same colour. What is more, the masks were different in each of the four pictures. In one Jagannath's eyes were almond shaped, in another he was doe-eyed, in another the eyes were red diamonds. It was the same with his nose. In one it was the large red outline of a cylinder broadened at the base, in another it was a small, black pear-drop with a little moustache beneath it. And it was the same with his brother and sister.

Now I began to understand the young *pande* when he said to me that Jagannath looks different to different people. The strands of pearls were so numerous and the garlands so broad that no neck or body was to be seen, and the colours of the clothes also varied from picture to picture. Of course they would do, for part of the elaborate ceremonial of the temple is the daily dressing and undressing of the idols. They themselves are, incredible as it may seem, simply logs of wood, hacked into the rough shape of head and bust. A small inset in the second picture showed me how the white one and the black one have crude arms projecting forward from the level of the ears.

A legend is told to account for the crudity of these rude totems. It is said that King Indradyumna went to Puri from Malwa to get hold of a sapphire image of Vishnu which was there, but just as he was about to seize it, it disappeared. Repenting of his covetousness he did penance and sacrificed a hundred horses. Whereupon he heard a heavenly voice saying that Vishnu would appear no longer as a sapphire but as a log of wood. The log, as promised, was found one day stranded on the beach and recognized by certain markings on it. Woodcarvers were then set to work to fashion the log into an image of Vishnu, but all they managed to do was to blunt their chisels. Then Vishnu, himself, appeared in the guise of an old carpenter, and said that he would do it if he was left alone and undisturbed with the log for three weeks. The king was too impatient. He broke into the room where the carpenter was working before the time was up, and found the three pieces of wood which are venerated today.

Even these three are not the originals, however. At certain times, decided by the astrologers, new images are made and installed with great ceremony. They are fashioned just as crudely as the old.

It may seem pointless to relate these fairy tales, but when one considers that the childlike activities connected with the three wooden dolls—the bathing, the dressing, the feeding, the entertaining—are carried out by a large number of people divided into nearly a hundred categories, who consider themselves to be at the heart of a religion professed by hundreds of millions of people, that both the high and mighty and the humble and meek have poured wealth at their feet, that even the famous Koh-i-Noor diamond was once bequeathed to them, and that the pronouncements of Puri are heard and weighed throughout India, it must be admitted that they have considerable significance. It may not be too fanciful to suggest that when the Bengalis saw their first white men, they thought as Montezuma thought of the Spaniards in Mexico, that the representatives of the god they saw at Puri had come to earth, and were for that reason eager to do their bidding.

I walked on down the broad road, the Baraband, and found the chariot under construction, that was to carry Jagannath to the garden temple in July. It is renewed each year and crowned with a tower 45 feet high, made of cloth on a bamboo framework, which represents the *deul* of the pagoda. This is the chariot, pulled by 4,000 men, that the Company's servants called the Juggernaut. It derived its sinister reputation from stories about people hurling themselves under its wheels to be crushed to death and gain a short cut to heaven. No doubt people were killed, but usually it was because of the pressure of the crowd, particularly as people believed that, if you could touch the image in the chariot, you would be freed from the cycle of rebirth.

Half way down the road was the lake with the white temple in it, to which Jagannath is taken in a decorated boat for a few weeks in the hot weather. It is his summer house, and nowadays he goes to the jetty on the lakeside by car. The garden temple is not much larger, and is his wife's house. Hence his visit there is matrimonial.

On the path in front of the temple some girls held out bunches of herbage to me, which they wanted me to buy in order to feed a cow that stood in front of me. I desisted, but the cow would not let me pass until I played the game, so I did what was required of me. Then there was the doorkeeper, wanting a rupee, for which he was willing to show me the frieze of the Krishna story on the wall, and both willing and eager to point out the friezes of erotica mixed in with it.

Inside the walls the layout was a replica of the Great Pagoda in miniature. At one end of the temple stood the three thrones of Jagannath and of his brother and sister, for they come too, riding lesser chariots, on the appointed day. At the other end of it stood Jagannath's wife—a black idol, dressed in patchwork clothes, with a sort of doll's toilet set and cosmetic necessities in front of her, and a fat *pande* demanding a donation.

This was the small part the non-Hindu could see, and I felt I had seen enough. Returning up the Baraband, I thought how childish these rituals, carried on in the great centres of Hinduism, are, and yet what a strong hold they still have on the people even in these days. They are the carry over of the ancient pagan world into modern times. Doubtless Diana of the Ephesians and Jupiter Ammon and the other great gods of the Roman world were tended in much the same fervent, elaborate way, and each temple had its own year of festivals developed according to the legends connected with it.

There are eighteen festivals at Puri, apart from the car festival, which attracts vast crowds from far and near. They are the rite of Spring, the destruction of the demon, the Florialia carnival of flowers, the elopement of the wife, the bathing, the lying up in sickness, the four months' sleep, the birthday, the slaying of the snake, and so on. And in each of them the log of wood is dressed up to take the part of the hero of the play. Thus Krishna, the mischievous boy, the great lover, the saviour of mankind, is brought into the minds of millions of simple people, who see in him both their own human clay and the divine. The *pandes*, who have seen it all time and again, collect the money and then send them off home.

Back amongst the traders' booths I watched a woman selling

brown medicines made from lizards, birds' beaks and snakes. Behind her, amongst the permanent shops lying back from the road, stood the Government Orissan Arts and Crafts Centre. I went inside. The assistant came forward. He thought he knew what I would be interested in. He showed me some cardboard circles, each about the size of a mat for a tumbler, handpainted with a green background and a yellow rim. Each one had a nude male figure in grey and a nude female figure in yellow on it, engaged in the varied art of copulation.

4

THE GATEWAY OF INDIA

I WENT back to Calcutta, and left India to return to Singapore and my army duties in Malaya. Shortly afterwards my tour in Malaya ended and I came home to England. My next visit to India was three years later. This time I arrived over the Arabian Sea instead of the Bay of Bengal after starting my flight at Zürich, but I had the same feeling of apprehensive curiosity as before.

In the years between much had happened. The cold war between India and Pakistan had flared up into a hot engagement on the western border. Pandit Nehru had died, and his successor as prime minister, Lalbahadur Shastri, after him. The general election had shaken the deep complacency of the Congress Party men, and the first serious famine since the Bengal disaster of 1942 had come to, of all places, Bihar, where millions of new acres were supposed to have been irrigated from the new Kosi river barrage and brought under cultivation.

The omens were not propitious. The rupee had been devalued from 13·4 to 20 to the pound, and India was once again holding out her begging bowl to the U.S.A. and other wealthier nations, as the juggernaut of her population explosion rolled on remorselessly.

From the moment that the big old De Soto taxi left Santa Cruz airport for the drive into Bombay the stench and poverty of the country hit me again like a blow in the face. Somehow I had expected Bombay, the queen of Indian cities, to be better. I had fondly tried to imagine that it was only in Calcutta where crowds of people were precariously living like rats in the bilges of a decayed old ship, that the other population centres would be different. But Bombay was the same. On either side of the road that I had once travelled daily into town there was a thick mass of hovels made of old kerosene tins and sacking, through which ran the huge water pipes from the Vehar and Tulsi reservoirs, which are the lifelines of the city. From the gaps in the clumps of these hovels rivulets of foul water ran between banks of green scum into the main tentacles of the creeks that remained from recent land reclamation.

It was dawn, and such a vile stench arose from these creeks and the hovels beside them that I could hardly get my breath. Beside the embankment of the road, as it rose towards the bridge crossing over to Mahim, there was a long row of men squatting down and excreting. Here and there, standing amongst the hovels, there were large, square, uncompleted apartment blocks, like posts put up in an ineffective attempt to hold back the rushing tide of humanity.

Of the Mahim causeway that I had known, only the bridge remained. The rest of the shallow inlets had been filled in, and rubble was still being tipped there to close the gap still further. On the eastern side, by Sion causeway, the gap had already been closed, so Bombay was no longer an island, it was simply a promontory of the large island of Salsette.

At Mahim the stink altered from sewage and excreta to fish as we passed the landing point for the primitive lug-sail fishing boats. It is graced with the name of "harbour", with a customs office attached, but it is no more than a banked-up shoreline, on which the catches are dumped amongst a line of shacks, which are surrounded by piles of sea shells.

At this early hour there was little traffic. My driver, presumably in order to conserve his petrol, showed an extreme reluctance to change gear, so we squelched around corners fast enough to be able to pick up again with a labouring, chattering engine, after rounding them, and trusting to providence that no early morning milkman with his yoked churns, or sleepy cow, or bullock cart would be in the way.

Thus we entered the city of Bombay, which was once a small trading port like Calcutta and Madras, but now heaves and swelters with a population of four million. In 1534, a quarter of a century after the Portuguese had conquered Goa, the Sultan of Gujerat ceded Bombay to them. More than a century later they handed it over to King Charles II as part of the dowry of his Portuguese queen on condition that he helped them against the Dutch. King Charles, in turn, handed it over to the East India Company to be rented for £10 per annum leasehold "as of the manor of East Greenwich".

The Portuguese probably did not reckon that they had lost much.

The seven small islands, surrounded by mud flats, which stank almost as much as the modern hovels on the road from Santa Cruz, were a malarious wilderness, and a man was reckoned lucky if he survived two monsoons. Until 1804, when the city was visited by the Duke of Wellington, or General Wellesley as he then was, there was not even a proper road up the Ghats to the interior. But the

Southern India

land was drained, the city became the Company's west coast head-quarters because of the security afforded by its island site, and in the nineteenth century it held the proud title of Urbs Prima in Indis—India's first city.

The old De Soto bucketed along the city streets and deposited me at my hotel, facing the wide harbour, just as the sun was coming up like a red light shining through the dusty air. I went inside and

5

spoke to the desk clerk on the night shift. Beside him there was a colourful poster of Kashmir and a bronze statue of the Dancing Siva, encircled by a ring of flames.

A difficulty arose. No reservation appeared to have been received.

"Some mistakes somewhere, I suppose," I said. "Anyway, perhaps you have a room."

He looked doubtful. "Without reservation very difficult."

"But my travel agent *was* supposed to make the reservation," I said. "It was through Hotel Plan. Look, I have the voucher."

"Yes, perhaps you have the voucher. But the voucher is not saying which hotel. I will have to ask the manager."

"There is a big sign at the airport," I said gently. "It says, 'Tourists are our honoured guests'. And there is another sign that says, 'Tourism—Passport to Peace'."

"I will see."

"Do you," I said, "happen to have a vacant room now?"

"There may be."

"Either there is or there isn't."

"Perhaps there will be."

"I am tired and I want to sleep."

"Certainly you may sleep."

"But how can I sleep if I haven't got a room?"

"Ah, that is another matter. I will see."

My taxi driver, who had come right into the hotel, was watching us and listening to the conversation with interest.

"I think you want to go somewhere else?" he said.

"I think I do," I said.

"I don't think so."

"I thought you said you do think so."

"I don't think you go," he said. "This is a very good hotel. First-class accommodation. Only two years they made it into a hotel."

"Perhaps there are two hotels with the same name."

"I think so."

"Let's go to the other one, then."

"I do not think there is another one."

"I thought you said you thought there was another one."

"There may be, but I do not know. You like to change money?"

"I'll go to the bank later."

"Change money in the bank? Nobody change money in the bank. I'll give you best rate."

"What is the best rate?"

"Rupees seven."

"Rupees seven what?"

"One dollar rupees seven."

"No. Pounds."

"Rupees twenty five. Change fifty pounds?"

"No. Not that much."

"Hundred pounds? I can do it."

"No."

"Best rate."

"Later."

"All right. Rupees twenty-six."

"But I've only got travellers' cheques. How can you change travellers' cheques?"

The taxi driver pulled a large wad of notes out of the back pocket of his grimy blue canvas trousers. "Doesn't matter travellers' cheques," he said. "I can do it. Let me see."

"Not now," I said.

"Rupees twenty-seven."

"I'll see."

I turned back to the desk clerk, who had been looking interminably up and down his list of reservations.

"Well, have you got a room?" I said.

"Perhaps I have one," he answered. "Temporary. Not first class accommodation."

"Never mind," I said. "I can sleep there."

The room was not first class, but it was adequate. If one opened the window one saw a little microcosm of an Indian village. There was a flame of the forest tree with its big red flowers in bloom, and below it men were sitting half naked on their hunkers, chattering together, getting up to go to a tap and pour water over themselves from a kerosene tin, rubbing their teeth with green twigs, and hawking and spitting into the open drain with that peculiarly raucous bubbling noise that I remembered in a flash as the Song of India. Two lean chickens were hopping about, pecking at the refuse on the bare, beaten earth, and a goat was worrying at the branches of a bush, trying to get at the leaves higher up. It was the world of the servants, that would never be seen from the permanently closed windows of the air-conditioned "first class accommodation".

I went to sleep, and when I awoke and got up again the sun was

high in the sky. Standing at the door of the hotel, I fumbled for
my dark glasses to protect my eyes from the glare. The doorkeeper,
dressed in khaki to give himself a kind of soldierly, efficient appear-
ance, leaped up. "Taxi?" he said.

A taxi driver, not ten yards away, leaned out of his car. "Taxi?"
he called.

"No, thank you. I'll walk."

They both looked puzzled by this mysterious decision, but
reluctantly let me go. I walked along the road beside the harbour.
According to the street sign it was named Premsing Jethsing
Ramchandani Marg, but it was still called Strand Road in the street
plan of the tourist pamphlet, and still, as I soon discovered, known
by everyone as Istrand Road. Further along to the left I could see
the domes and towers of the famous Taj Mahal Hotel, and on the
right, standing out into the sea, was the Gateway of India.

A low wall separated the promenade of Strand Road from the
sea, and daubed along the whole length of it were the remains of the
campaign slogans for the general election. "Manohar Kotwal,
symbol hut", followed by the crude white outline of a hut, alternated with "George Fernandes, symbol tree", followed by a daub of
a tree. Across the road the remnants of a poster clung to a gatepost:

WAR ON POVERTY

Vote for Independent

K. T. MIRCHANDANI

Alias BHAGWANDAS T. M.
Lok Sabha (House of People)
Bombay South Constituency

1. Houses for all. 2. Food, clothing, medical aid guaranteed. 3. Instan-
taneous justice. 4. No permits. Free Trade. 5. Telephone. 6. Revalua-
tion. Symbol—Lion.

I wondered how Mr Mirchandani had been going to provide
houses for all, and guarantee medical aid, and overcome the law's
delays. Had he been going to provide a telephone for everyone, or
only for the chosen few? And why did he need an alias?

Perhaps we shall never know, for George Fernandes, the man with
the Portuguese name, won a resounding victory in Bombay South
and became the "giant-killer" who defeated S. K. Patel, the un-
crowned Congress king of Bombay. He united the poor behind him
with his promises to fight for better housing, slum clearance and

improved water supplies, and perhaps it was easier for him, a Goanese, to unite Maharashtrians and Gujeratis, Hindus and Muslims, in a joint protest against the existing powers.

The result in Bombay North-east was just as startling, for the saturnine V. K. Krishna Menon, who had been a key man in the Congress Party as Indian representative to the United Nations and as Defence Minister, was not adopted. In his place S. G. Barve, who could look back on a distinguished career in the Indian Civil Service, went to Delhi. When he died a month later there was widespread mourning in the city.

These were but two examples of the sweeping swing away from the Congress Party establishment, which characterized the election results. India has the largest electorate in the world, and one of the least educated. There were 250 million voters in the general election of 1967, voting for candidates to fill 520 seats in the Lok Sabha, the People's Assembly. The Congress Party won a bare majority in contrast with their overwhelming numerical superiority in the previous government. The President of the party, Mr Kamaraj, was himself defeated, as well as more than a dozen ministers.

In the simultaneous elections for the seventeen states Congress lost their majority in seven. Their outstanding defeats were in Madras to the waxing Dravidian party of the South and, for the second time, in Kerala to the Communists. Other parties, too, have been rising to the surface to break the hegemony of the party which led India to independence. The Swatantra party, led by the veteran politician, C. P. Rajagopalachari, is supported by conservative elements and is strong in the former princely states of Rajasthan, but most prominent amongst them is the Jan Sangh, which appeals to the deepest roots of reactionary Hinduism. It campaigns for a nation-wide ban on the killing of cows, for a Hindu rather than a secular India, "selling to the harassed people," as Baburao Patel says in his magazine, *Mother India*, "the ancient but beautiful dream of Hindu Rashtra, which once made this country a land of milk and honey."

Alas it has been a dream for a long time, for over 150 years ago the Abbé Dubois was lamenting the poverty of the Hindus. "India," he said, "has always been considered a most wealthy and opulent country, a land literally flowing with milk and honey." He mentions the fabulous diamonds of Golconda, the delicate muslins, fine cloths and beautiful cottons, and adds that "those who, after visiting the country, have dared to affirm that India is the poorest and most wretched of all the civilized countries of the world, have simply not been believed".

The dream still continues in the tourist pamphlets, and in the travellers' tales of lavish tiger shoots and of vast entertainments in maharajas' palaces, of opulent race-goers and hectic gamblers. But it is wearing thin. The reality stares at one every week from the pages of the English Sunday newspapers in the form of a little, dark child, with matchstick arms and legs and a belly that looks unnaturally swollen in comparison. It stares at one more starkly in England than in India itself, for no such picture is to be seen in Indian newspapers, and under the blind sun in the land of its birth, the starving child seems to be clad with the magic cloak of invisibility.

Even so it was not surprising that the voters, the majority of whom are the poor and hungry, should turn away from the party that had grown fat itself without being able to fill the bellies of its supporters. Yet some Congress leaders could not believe that the reaction against their party was spontaneous and were convinced that the American Central Intelligence Agency was behind it, just as it had been proved to have been behind the overthrow of Dr Jagan's Indian party in Guyana. The notoriously anti-American Bombay weekly, *Blitz,* even claimed that the Congress President had been defeated by U.S. dollars in his constituency near Madurai in the far South, and that Mrs Joshi had suffered a like fate near Lucknow.

Such accusations have the flavour of excuses. At the same time there does exist a sinister side to Indian politics, often allied to the extraordinary and bizarre. In November 1966, on a day that has since become known as Black Friday, thousands of naked devotees of Siva appeared in the nation's capital. These *saddhus,* who were estimated to be no less than 200,000 strong, rioted in protest against the lack of legislation forbidding the slaughter of cows in all the states instead of in only nine. They sacked and fired ministers' houses and broke into the Congress President's home bent on murder.

Kamaraj escaped with his life. Next month, addressing a meeting in the southern town of Salem, he accused the big capitalists of North India of trying to engineer his destruction because of his Socialist policies. "They want to remove me from their path," he said, "Desperate, they resorted to foul means on November 7th." He cannot have forgotten that Mahatma Gandhi was murdered by a Hindu extremist of the Rashtriya Swayam Sewak Sangh, the National Volunteer Organization, which is now under the wing of the Jan Sangh. Sporadic violence from the overtly direct action Siva Sena, the Army of Siva, was also reported in Bombay and other places at election time.

Some responsible commentators, indeed, have seriously doubted whether parliamentary democracy will survive any longer in India against the pulls of faction and caste. Neville Maxwell, writing from Delhi for *The Times* of London, was convinced that this would be the last general election to be held, and I was reminded of his words as I walked alongside the low sea wall in Strand Road, Bombay. If this were so, I was sure that these election slogans, daubed all over Bombay so permanently in white paint, would survive far longer than the free elections that had occasioned them. Like the Sketches by Boz and the sporting prints still hanging in the clubs, Manohar Kotwal, symbol hut, and George Fernandes, symbol tree, would remain as the mantric formulae of a superseded age.

"Change money? Excuse me. You want to change money?"

Unnoticed a young man had fallen into step with me and kept pace with me as I walked along.

"How much?" I said.

"Six."

"No. Pounds, not dollars."

"Twenty-four."

"That's no good. I was offered twenty-seven last night."

"How much you want to change?"

"I'm not sure."

"Thirty?"

"Perhaps more than that."

"Twenty? I changing any number you like."

"I'll see later."

"Change now. No good later. Best rate now."

"Maybe better rate later."

"No. Change now."

"Later."

"All right. You wanting changing money just going there by that big archway."

"The Gateway of India?"

"Asking for Purushottam Das. You want postcards?"

"Maybe."

"You just ask for Purushottam Das."

"Yes. Thank you."

I walked on past the Taj Mahal Hotel and into the city.

"Sir. Please, Sir." A small boy was running alongside me. "Give me money, Sir."

Remembering the past, I made no answer.

"Poor boy, Sir. Please, Sir."

The voice whined insidiously. The little feet pattered along beside me. I thought what a hard man I must be to make no answer. The rich white man could so easily give something, and yet there were brown men passing doubtless richer than me.

"You give me money." The little boy ran on ahead, turned and confronted me. I had to either walk into him or step aside. Turning myself, like the Indians, into a blind man, I walked on.

The little hand tapped my arm. "You give. Come on, you give!" It was an order now. It was an official demanding his customs dues.

I still said nothing. Once again the little boy ran ahead. This time he not only stood in my way, as he had done before, he threw himself at my feet and banged his head on my shoes.

It was his last ploy. At the Colaba road-turning he stopped as suddenly as he had started, having reached the end of his beat. On the next stretch, opposite the Prince of Wales Museum, a woman with a baby on her arm took over. I envied the brown men, for they were left unmolested, while a white face drew the beggars like a magnet. Walking became a misery. One could not stop to look at a building or a shop window without being insistently accosted. The desire to escape became irresistible. I thought of the look the hotel doorkeeper had given me when I had told him I was going to walk, and I began to understand.

The red double-decker buses were churning their ways round the Wellington Fountain, which was put up in the mid-nineteenth century to commemorate the Iron Duke's connection with the city. They looked oddly English, belonging, like the old cars that were still on the road, to twenty years ago. They were England with strange signs in Hindi and Gujerati slapped on to them, England with a strange background of domes and minarets, amongst people

who spoke English in such a strange way that they were often almost
incomprehensible.

I looked up at a poster on the wall beside me. "Use taxy only
when you must. Otherwise avoid. Taxy users association." So I had
been right to walk after all.

A plump, balding, dark man came bustling alongside me,
balancing his umbrella on his fingers. "How do you like Bombay?"
he said. "Bloody government. Ah, the British time! You, British?
Yes? Oh, the British time was marvellous. My wife is from Liver-
pool. I work in the customs here, but it so happens I have a holiday
today. How lucky. God meant it like that, so that I can have the
pleasure of meeting you. My daughter is in America—Philadelphia.
Of course the foreign exchange problem. . . ."

"I knew it! Change money?"

"As a friend. I could come to your hotel. How lucky I have a
holiday today."

Escape to sanctuary. That is what, sooner or later, one is forced
to do in every Indian city. I escaped from Mahatma Gandhi Road,
the former Esplanade, into the doorway of the Prince of Wales
Museum.

Constructed in the nineteenth century Mogul style, like many of
the imposing public buildings of Bombay, the pale blue-grey dome
is set in the middle of a fringe of miniature minarets built of the
local yellow basalt. If the dome of the museum had been bright
blue instead, it might have been in Persia, and it was indeed a
sanctuary. Long-eared black bronze Buddhas stood serenely beside
the clipped hedgerows of the walks. Jackdaws cawed to each other
in the palm trees, and one was perched on the Wolseley helmet of
the statue of King George V as Prince of Wales. It was in just such
a helmet that I had first arrived in India at the Bombay docks. I had
lost it when we were issued with the new lighter pith helmets at the
Officer Cadet School in Mhow, yet King George's helmet still
remains, stained white as snow by the droppings of the jackdaws,
and the motto *Ich Dien*, "I serve", can still be read on the pedestal
below.

The great halls of the museum were cool and uncrowded, but I
did not stay long. In a small annex to the left of the main building
a modern art exhibition was being held, which interested me more
than the traditional exhibits. It was a collection of sculpture made
mainly out of blocks, sheets and rods of metal welded together. In

some the metal sheets were solid, and in others they were a grid of squares or circles. In some large pebble stones had been incorporated to represent, perhaps, a head or a limb.

Each sculpture gave some vague indication of a figure or an idea, but it was usually necessary to consult the catalogue card to get at what had actually been in the mind of the sculptor. One piece was mainly composed of a forest of metal sheets and was called "Room Divided". Another, made largely of rods and blocks, was named "The Warrior". "The Buddha" had a motor-car engine bracket for a body and a large steel nut for a head. One, with presumably no basic underlying idea at all, was simply called "Stone and Steel", but two others were essays in stylised movement and named after the two best-known modes of Indian dancing—the Bharat Natyam and the Kathakali. They were certainly extremely avant-garde and in complete contrast with the specimens in the museum. Clearly the inspiration was from the West.

It was not surprising, then, that the sculptor, Pilloo R. Pochkhanawala, had a Parsi name, for the Parsis have always been amongst the most westernized and forward-looking races of India, and it was in Bombay that they first gained prominence and power.

The Parsis originally came from Persia, whence they fled in the eighth century, when the Muslims persecuted their Zoroastrian religion and destroyed their fire temples. But the Muslims followed them to the eastern seaboard of India in the sixteenth century, and they did not really prosper until the British occupation brought religious tolerance. They still have their fire temples in Bombay, and visitors are taken to see the Towers of Silence on Malabar Hill, where the vultures pick clean the bodies of the dead, but it is for far more than this that they are known in India today. With the great Parsi family of Tata they have been the leaders of India's industrialization. The big steel town of Tatanagar in the East carries their name, and Dr Homi Babha, a world renowned atomic scientist who died tragically in a plane crash on Mont Blanc, was one of their most brilliant sons.

Miss Pochkhanawala was talking about her sculptures. "I go to a factory to get all these bits of metal," she said. "They call it scrap. Some people don't understand these sculptures, but you know, I have a class of deaf and dumb children I teach, and I brought them round without saying anything to them, and do you know, one of the little girls was standing in front of this one, the Kathakali, and she actually began to do a kind of dance. Isn't that amazing?"

I looked at the piece again, and it was strange how the crude shapes of metal that were welded together—the forked head, the shapeless arms—did have a sort of primitive evocative power. I thought of the crude dolls at Puri, that move millions into a passion of devotion. Perhaps the very crudity is the power, leaving the imagination free to work.

Outside, the heat had built up too great a pressure for me to support on my first day in the tropics, so I hurried back to my hotel on the seafront for lunch and a siesta. Elephanta Island, with its ancient caves containing the massive graven gods of the Hindus, had disappeared into the glare, and Strand Road was deserted except for George Fernandes and Manohar Kotwal.

Up in the new air-conditioned room, into which I had now moved, I studied the notice in red print in my bathroom:

Patrons residing in the hotel are requested not to allow consumption of Alcohol by friends in their rooms except after satisfying themselves that all persons drinking Alcohol are Permit-Holders, under any of the following classes of permits:
1. Special permits to foreign Sovereigns etc.
2. Visitor's permits and
3. Interim permits.

Could these have been the permits that K. T. Mirchandani, alias Bhagwandas T. M., had promised to abolish in his election manifesto? I might have obtained a Visitor's Permit at the airport if I had not felt too tired to delay any longer and decided that the bottle of Scotch I had bought at Djibouti for fifteen shillings would have to be enough. But what was an Interim Permit?

These musings brought to my mind the whole question of Prohibition, which looms so large in the conversation of Europeans in India. It is a state matter. Some states are dry and others are not. Furthermore, in some states liquor is reasonably priced, but in others it is taxed so highly that few people can afford to drink. For instance, in Mysore a litre bottle of beer costs Rupees 3·50 in the hotels, but in neighbouring Kerala the price is Rupees 7·50. Maharashtra, the state created out of parts of the Bombay Presidency, Hyderabad and the Central Provinces, is dry. The little toddy shops that used to be dotted about the city streets, have been hopefully transformed into Government Milk Centres. To drink the forbidden liquor the law says that you must either be a foreign visitor or need it for medical reasons, and the pegs of whisky and bottles of beer must be marked off on your permit card as they are drunk.

It is easy to see that there will be ways round this law, and when the All-India Prohibition Council produced a report in 1967, it was almost a cry of despair. It blamed "drinking officers of the Government" for being the main obstacle to efficient enforcement of Prohibition, and complained succinctly that "a dry law cannot be enforced if the agency is manned by wets". It also tilted at the army, alleging that "immoderate drinking exists among officers", and in addition affirmed that "extensive illicit distillation is carried on throughout the country".

Reading this sorry stuff, one is tempted to ask why the Governments persist in Prohibition. Have they forgotten the lesson of the U.S.A., or have they still some racial memory of the British master-race swaggering out of their clubs full of liquor and insulting the Indians in their way, or are they really concerned about the health and efficiency of the community? When I was stationed at Marol in a camp tucked away in the jungle on Salsette Island, we well knew that the local villagers were active distillers of liquor for sale in Bombay. Presumably the situation has not much changed. Those who want liquor badly enough will get it, but it will probably be worse liquor because it cannot be drunk openly.

The sun was down behind the row of high buildings when I emerged once more from my hotel, and Strand Road was populated once again. I walked down to the Gateway of India on Apollo pier. In the old days it was as well-known to the British as the Taj Mahal at Agra, for in the days of sea travel the majority entered India through Bombay. They could hardly avoid seeing it, though it was the actual landing place only for V.I.P.s. Other passengers on the liners had to go through to the customs on Ballard pier.

The Gateway was built in honour of the greatest V.I.P. of all, to commemorate the visit of the Emperor of India, King George V, and Queen Mary in 1911, but as an afterthought, not for their actual use. Like small fish under the protection of the great whale, statues subsequently sprung up beside it. On one side stands Hardinge of Penshurst, a long way from his pleasant place in the Weald of Kent, who was Viceroy during the First World War.

Beyond him stands the King himself, hewn by an Indian sculptor.
No hand has toppled them in the fervour of Independence, but as
if to balance the record, a new statue of Sivaji, the Mahratta hero
of the seventeenth century, was added in 1960.

Sivaji, whose base was at Poona, rebelled against his Moslem
rulers, uniting all classes in freedom from the Brahmins' controls.
His fame went down in history and in the folk songs of Maharashtra
as a great Hindu patriot, and so his name, which is the same as that
of their great god, was adopted as a rallying cry for the Hindus of
the Independence Movement.

The yellow basalt of the Mogul style gateway looked golden in the
late afternoon sunlight. Beyond it the broad expanse of the harbour
was dotted with shipping, including some grey corvettes of the
Indian Navy, and to the left yachts lay at smaller moorings closer
inshore in front of what used to be the clubhouse and grounds of the
Royal Bombay Yacht Club.

The clubhouse is now in the hands of the Government of India
Atomic Energy Department for reasons that can hardly be considered a functional necessity. But Indians, as a whole, are not much
interested in sailing as a sport, and the Yacht Club was one of the
strongholds of white supremacy until the Indian Navy took it over
shortly after Independence, so perhaps it was inevitable that this
magnificent site should fall into the hands of the government
bureaucrats. The Yacht Club itself survives without the epithet
"royal" in different premises across the road, and occasionally lays
on a party in the small "permit room" when members can be
persuaded to surrender a portion of their alcohol ration to the
common cause.

From the landing stage near the former Yacht Club people were
embarking on one of the old lug-sail boats for a trip around the
harbour. They were mostly women and children, using it as a
means of getting a breath of cool air off the water, and I left them at
it. Up above on the pier, tucked in close to the great hall of the
Gateway, vendors of roasted peanuts, chick-peas and tiny fried
noodles were sitting behind their stalls. Another street vendor was
standing beside his machine for crushing sugar-cane, and another
was ready with his hatchet to slice off the top of a fresh coconut.
On the seaward side sat the sellers of postcards, envelopes and
pens. "Change money?" one said softly as I passed. It was Purushottam Das.

Further down Apollo Pier Road sat the *pan* sellers, with elaborate, shining brass trays of *pan* leaves, lime and betel nut, and other flavouring ingredients for the delights of chewing. One of them wanted to prepare a leaf for me, but my courage failed me and he did not press the point. He was more interested in playing with a white child that a nursemaid, belonging to one of the Himalayan hill tribes, had brought along for his evening airing.

A child beggar attacked me as I skirted round the grounds of the Bombay Legislature Council Chamber, observed approvingly by her mother, who was squatting against the railings. I thought of darting inside, but a notice saying, "The public are warned to refrain from using this compound as a passage" deterred me. Another beggar approached—a man with one arm—and he was pushed into the gutter by a dark man with two arms saying, "Change money," and he in his turn was elbowed aside by a wiry little man, with a wrinkled, yellow, narrow-eyed face, wearing a dark suit and a khaki topi of the kind nowadays usually restricted to ice-cream vendors.

"Very hot!" he said. "I imagine you are not used to so much heat. My name is John Macdonald, and you are British. I can see that."

"How do you know I'm British?"

"Very easy. I can tell the British when I see them."

"People think we're Americans these days."

"Not me. I can always tell the British. I served with the British in the army. I think you'd like a drink of beer or a peg of whisky."

"Yes, I would."

"Why wouldn't you like a drink?"

"But I said I would."

"Oh, I thought you would. I could see it."

"But I haven't got a permit card."

"You are British, I think. You've been in the army?"

"Yes."

"Never mind the permit then. You drink with me. Old comrades. We'll take a taxi."

John held out his hand to stop a taxi, took his hat off and got inside. I followed him. We drove past a cinema plastered with a huge poster of James Bond's head and gun facing us over the middle of an outstretched naked, golden, female body, advertising the film "Goldfinger".

"They never thought of that one for the temple carvings," I said.

John Macdonald did not answer. He was busy directing the driver. We passed a rash of great new buildings, built on land not long ago reclaimed from the sea. Unlike the noble brown and red buildings of the beginning of the century, which are now half obscured amidst the dust and bustle and telegraph wires and apartment blocks of the city, these stood out white and virginal in their treeless grounds.

There was the huge honeycomb of the Sachivalaya—the Maharashtra Secretariat. "Full air-conditioning," said John. "Everyone wants to get a job in there." Next to it stood the main building of the India Life Insurance Company, a government enterprise, which is attempting to bring social security to a wide base of the people. Beyond that the enormous name-plate of Esso Oil rose above the flat roof of another big office block.

Past Esso we reached the long, curving sweep of Back Bay, with the rising ground of Malabar Hill enclosing it on the far side. Netaji Subhash Road, named after Subhashchandra Bose, who fought on the Japanese side in the Second World War, runs its whole length, but everyone still knows it as Marine Drive.

"I expect you're wondering why I've got such a funny face," John Macdonald said.

"No," I answered. "I'm not wondering why you've got a funny face."

"Well, I'll tell you," he said. "My mother was a Japanese."

"Oh, I see."

"My father was British, of course. He was in the Black Watch."

"He would be with a name like that," I said.

"I was in the army during the war. Jubbulpore."

"You were in a difficult position, then."

"Why?"

"Your mother being a Japanese."

"Oh not at all, man. I knew which side I was on. I was on the side of the British."

"You're a sort of Anglo-Indian with a difference, then. What's happened to all the Anglo-Indians now? They used to run the railways and the police and do all kinds of useful things."

"Oh, they've all gone home now."

"Home to Britain?"

"Yes, mostly. They couldn't carry on, you see. Getting squeezed out and not getting promotion. So they went home."

"They always called Britain 'home', even the ones that had never been there."

"It was too difficult for them to stay. They had to learn to do their own cooking and housework and go home."

"But you stayed."

"I've got my job here, but just today I have a holiday."

Round the back of Netaji Subhash Road, alias Marine Drive, John called to the driver to stop. We got out and walked down to a high, ten-storey apartment block that was being built out of re-inforced concrete. A trellis work of bamboo scaffolding surrounded it, and rough tree-trunks stood like pit-props between the over-hanging balconies, to be knocked away when the concrete was set. Not a single crane or concrete-mixer or conveyor-belt was to be seen. Women stirred the cement and sand together by hand, and a relay of men, one standing on each balcony, passed the building material up from their feet to their heads to get it to the top.

"They'll be finishing work now," John said. "Don't worry."

"I'm not worried," I said. "But where are we going?"

"They're all my friends here. Comrades."

"I see. A speakeasy."

"No one will worry us here. The inspector's my friend."

"I'm not worried," I said. "I'm a tourist. It's International Tourist Year."

"You don't have to worry, man."

"But I told you, I'm not worried."

The basement of the building had already been divided into rooms, and into one of these we went. The walls were of bare concrete, and the floor was covered with a fine dust of cement, which rose in little puffs of smoke as we walked. There were three chairs, a bare table and a naked electric light bulb suspended on a dust-whitened flex in the centre of the room.

A beady-eyed man, dressed in a white shirt and khaki shorts, poked his head through the gap where there was going to be a door.

"Get us a drink, Moti," said John.

"You want a peg?"

"A peg of what?" I said.

"Whisky."

"No. Beer."

Konarak—lovers

Konarak—the Sun God

Puri—entrance to the
White Pagoda

"I'll get you some whisky."

"But I said I'd like beer."

"Old comrades. Better drink whisky."

"Old comrades can drink beer," I said.

"O.K., man. Moti, get the beer."

Moti looked at me with beady dog eyes. "Why you not drinking whisky?"

"I like beer," I said.

"O.K., Moti," said John Macdonald. "Get the beer. And make sure the glasses are clean. This is a good friend."

"Pay now," said Moti.

"All right," I said. I parted with seven rupees and 25 new paisa. The 25 paisa were presumably added on to make it look like a genuine price.

In a minute Moti returned with a litre bottle of Bangalore beer and two thick, opaque glasses.

"*Achchha!*" said John. He took a glass, placed it in my hand and poured the beer. He did the same for himself. "Cheerio!" he said.

I wanted to laugh at such a ridiculous performance to get a glass of beer, but it was no laughing matter for John Macdonald. He drank and sucked his breath in through his teeth in a solemn ritual, and went on talking about the great days when he was attached to the Black Watch.

Meanwhile the building workers left, and three or four more men came into the speakeasy. But instead of beer they drank a colourless arak, which John said was a local distillation. "Don't worry," he said again. "The inspector is a friend."

The arak drinkers were also solemn over their drinking, and screwed up their mouths at the unpleasant taste when they sipped the spirit. Yet still it went down, like a drug that tastes foul but is supposed to do you good. They were quite silent, in contrast with the usual volubility of Indians, but that may have been because I was there.

Altogether this secret drinking place was a melancholy by-product of the prohibition laws, and I was far from keen to stay long. I told John I was going. "What about the gay girls?" he said hopefully. "I know some really gay girls. Make you feel like the good old days."

"Thank you very much, but I don't feel like the gay girls just now," I said. I had to fight his resistance to get away, but there was a reason for my resolve. I wanted to book a flight to Goa for the

6

next day, and I had to get to the Indian Airlines office in Mahatma Gandhi Road before it closed. This I just managed to do. For once I was pleasantly surprised by the extreme efficiency with which the reservations officer dealt with my request. Besides handling two constantly ringing telephones, he booked my flight with military precision, spelling out my name—Father, Orange, Roger, Bitter, Easy, Sugar—and writing out my ticket for me, all in the space of five minutes.

Back in the hotel there was still time to spare after a shower and a change of clothes before the evening meal, for in India they serve dinner late in the hotels, following the Sahibs' tradition, and usually one cannot start before eight o'clock. I sat with the Bombay newspaper, reading the matrimonial column, and strange reading it was. Whatever the official view of caste may be, it was obvious that in the intimate business of selecting a marriage partner it is still of considerable importance, together with the predictions of astrology.

"Wanted," one advertisement read. "An accomplished girl in the age group 19–24 from an affluent Brahmin family of status, Telegu or Tamil, to marry a young South Indian Telegu Brahmin graduate earning over Rs 1,200 per month in the private sector."

And another: "Handsome Buddhist youth, Baniya caste, director of two firms and property worth about five lakhs (i.e. 500,000) seeks a good charactered, educated, beautiful girl, who can speak English, with a reasonable dowry, within the age of 18 to 22 years. Please enclose horoscope copy and photograph."

In yet another a suitable match is wanted "for matriculate *khatri* beautiful girl of 22. Father's income four figures. Early marriage". A fourth advertiser, a "double graduate Catholic bachelor, high income, good capital, 35", wants a "fair graduate Goan Catholic girl".

And so it goes on, matching caste and horoscope and dowry, and hoping for beauty as well. Another column is devoted to astrology— astrological consultations, rectification of horoscopes, astrological guidance, and annual directions for 1967, with the warning that "this is a tricky year".

It may well be as tricky a year as any other, I thought to myself as I went in to dinner. The dining-room manager took my order and passed it to the head "bearer", who, in turn, passed it on to one of his assistants, who in turn passed it to an apprentice boy, who went out to the kitchen. As there was no choice on the menu, it seemed rather a superfluous procedure.

After dinner I went out again. It was only nine o'clock, yet the traffic was so sparse that the main roads looked as wide as landing strips on an airfield. I took a taxi into the middle of the city, driving down to the end of Mahatma Gandhi Road and into Parel Road. We then turned left into Grant Road—the one that Kipling mentions in McAlister's hymn. Judging by the potholed side roads and the crumbling buildings and the dust rising from the people's feet, one would have thought that it was still recovering from an air raid, if one did not know that Bombay had never been bombed.

It was impossible to go into the side turnings, for they were blocked by rows of long shapes under grey sheets that looked like corpses laid out ready to be taken to the mortuary. But they were not corpses, they were living people, for whom there was no room to sleep inside the buildings without suffocating heat and over-crowding. On some stretches there were shop fronts with iron grills in front of them, behind which the poor sisters of the gay girls waited for business calls. In the parallel road to the north the grounds of the former Byculla Club, that had been famous and exclusive in the days of the British Raj, were occupied by a mass of lorries parked in the State Transport Terminal.

Back in the down-town area of Mahatma Gandhi Road and Dadabhai Naoroji, alias Hornby Road, and out of the inferno of crowded poverty that I had just been through, the roads lay silent and empty with hardly a vehicle to be seen. Yet it was only half past nine.

5

THE APOSTLE OF THE INDIES

I CAUGHT the plane for Goa with the full approval of the hotel receptionist, who was a Goanese himself. "It's a good place for cashew nuts," he said, as a sweeper woman stirred up the dust on the floor between us with a little broom made of a bundle of blades of grass. "They make a liqueur out of them."

But it was for more than nuts that I was going there. Goa was forcibly taken over by the Indian Republic in 1961, after having been Portuguese for 450 years, and I wanted to see how this place, where Europeans had been making history for a hundred years before the British came on the scene, was faring under her new masters.

The flight in the Viscount was smooth and comfortable. The announcements were made first in Hindi, the national language in spite of the objections of the South, and then in English, and a fish lunch was served as a safe way through the various objections of various religions to different kinds of meat. I followed the gaze of two white-turbaned Sikhs who were looking out of their window, and saw Bombay laid out end to end from Salsette Island to the long finger of Colaba Causeway pointing out to the lighthouse at the southernmost land's end. On big stretches of the foreshore a patch-work of white on black showed where the washermen had spread out the city's bedsheets to dry on the stone embankments. It seemed a terrible waste of miles of esplanade that could have been turned into a marina for the citizens.

We headed south along the Konkan coast—a bare and empty shore, punctuated at intervals by old forts perched on offshore islands. These were the strong points, into which the coastwise traffic of the European traders would retire in times of stress, when the mainland was unsafe. Tavernier describes the route from Surat, 170 miles north of Bombay, to Goa, 250 miles to the south, as it was in Mogul times in the seventeenth century.

The land route was so difficult and dangerous that men went by sea, rowed all the way in stages varying from twenty-five to sixty-five miles. The first stage was from Surat, the point of departure for the Mogul court at Agra, to Daman, the second from Daman, which was still a Portuguese enclave until 1961, to Bassein at the top end of Salsette Island, the third from Bassein to Chaul, across the harbour from Bombay, when there was still nothing at Bombay except for coconuts, and the next four stages were down the coast over which we were flying.

The forts frequently changed hands in the fighting between the Portuguese and the Dutch, until the British won through over both. Then, with the advent of modern transport, they lost their importance. Seen from the aircraft they looked as though they had been baked and frazzled in the hot sun of centuries, and withered like the dead branches of a tree that was once full of sap. Behind them, just visible in the heat haze, lay the long rampart of the Western Ghats.

We reached Dabolim, the airport for Goa, in the early afternoon. But there was a long delay waiting for the ferry, which takes one over the Zuari river to the island on which both Old Goa and Panjim, the modern capital of the Goa territory, stand. I was sharing a Mercedes taxi with an architect, who had graduated from the Bombay School of Architecture made famous in the East by Wittet, the designer of the Gateway of India.

He regaled me with grim stories of how prices had shot up in Goa after the Indian takeover. The price of rice, which the Portuguese had subsidized, had gone up many times, he said. Bananas he claimed to be six times as expensive because they were now being collected for export. I thought he exaggerated, but he obviously enjoyed telling his tale of the troubles of Goa so much that I did not like to stop him. When he came to describe the consignment of bananas sent under government auspices to Italy, which had been found to be so rotten on arrival that all the fruit had to be packed into plastic bags and destroyed, he seemed positively delighted.

We moved forward to board the ramshackle ferry, that takes only four cars at a time, but the bishop's limousine arrived at that moment and jumped the queue. We had to wait again. The spastic beggar, who had accosted us at the beginning of our wait, came forward a second time to try his luck once more. The ferry returned, and at last we were aboard.

During the drive of fifteen miles to Panjim the taxi driver added to the tale of rising prices. His secondhand Mercedes was now worth 40,000 rupees, he said, which is £2,000 even at the exchange rate of the devalued rupee. I asked why Goa had not wanted to join Maharashtra state and preferred to remain under the direct rule of Delhi.

"Regionalism," the architect averred. "Regionalism, the curse of India. They feel they're quite different from the people of Maharashtra—the Mahrattas and Gujeratis and so on."

"I think there is another reason that the newspaper commentators don't mention," I said. "Maharashtra is dry. Can you imagine the Goanese living without their liquor?"

He laughed. "That is another reason," he said. "Although Bandodkar promised that Goa wouldn't go dry, they didn't believe him. They say there's still a lot of people living on the profit from liquor import permits granted at the time of the Pope's visit to Bombay."

It was late afternoon before we arrived at the hotel overlooking the Mandovi river on the other side of the island, and the architect and I parted company. I had great expectations, and looked forward to a good dinner, for the Goanese are renowned throughout India as cooks, and are well known on the P. and O. ships that ply the sea routes between Britain and the East. But first there was still time to see the town before nightfall.

At first sight Panjim looked like any other Indian urban centre, with its blocks of little shops with open fronts and living accommodation above, its crumbling pavements, its bicycles and its rattling single decker buses, but of course there was a difference. For a start the names of the streets and the company offices were in Portuguese, and advertisements on the walls encouraged one to drink Hercules brandy and Highland whisky.

The Avenida Vasco da Gama led along the river front past the treasury of the "Islands of Goa, Daman and Diu," which was guarded by armed soldiers and faced a flagpole flying the flag of the Indian Republic as if to emphasize the recent conquest. In the municipal gardens, which form the central square of the town, Indian music was alternating with rock 'n roll for the entertainment of the public, and at the far end of it stood a column carrying a statue to that same Vasco da Gama, who discovered the sea route to India round the Cape of Good Hope in 1498. The plaques of

Afonso de Albuquerque's head on the front, and of Luis de Camoens on the back of the plinth supporting the column completed the trinity of discoverer, conqueror and narrator, for Albuquerque seized Goa from the King of Bijapur's domains in 1510, and the poet commemorated the conquest in the famous epic of the Lusiads.

In one of the corners of the square there were some odd little huts, which smacked of petty governmental and philanthropic activity. One was the Government of Goa, Daman and Diu milk distribution centre, another was the gift shop of the National Council of Women in India, and a third called itself the Centre of Latin Culture (Centro de Cultura Latina). They looked so small and shabby that one wondered what could ever go on inside them, what gifts the women would offer and who would go there to seek culture, but round the corner of the next block a sudden apparition faced me, which showed me that there was at least something in Goa as I had imagined it after all.

The white church of Our Lady of the Immaculate Conception, with the big silver bell in its central tower, stood like a wedding cake at the top of a series of terraces with steps zigzagging up to the forecourt. Over the main door the virgin and child looked down, with the mystic sign *Ora pro Nobis* above. Some young men ran up the steps to be in time for mass, and a group of girls hurried past, with little black cambric scarves over their heads to symbolize veils. The mass began, the chanted responses swelled out of the building into the still evening air, intense with passionate religiosity, and I peeped inside. The church was nearly full, for almost half of Goa's 600,000 people are Christians. Beside the door there were little booklets for the faithful to buy for a few paisa. One was called, "Ten faults of husbands", and another, "Ten faults of wives", and a third entitled, "Kissing. Replies to constant queries."

It was certainly down to earth material, for kissing is not yet regarded so lightly in India as it is in most of Europe. To some a kiss on the mouth is really regarded as part of the sex act, to others it is just obscene, but the moderns, who see kisses scattered like daisies through the films of the western world that come to their cinemas, are unable to consider them so seriously. So the question then arises as to how lightly they may be given. Can one kiss anyone in the way of social greeting, or only one's fiancé, or only one's husband or wife? It is perplexing, so the Church, which watches over everything from the cradle to the grave, steps in to give advice.

A group of nuns walked past—dark faces in white robes. Then I returned to my hotel with a growing appetite for the products of Goanese cooking. Up in my room I read the notice to guests, which said, "Service charge 10 per cent, Sales tax 5 per cent. The guests are kindly requested not to encourage the tip system." This was, indeed, a reversal of the time-honoured Indian tradition of bestowal of *bakshish* on servants and retainers. Rule 13 was another break with tradition that I had not seen before: "The guests are required to deposit a certain sum as guarantee for board and lodging." I had evidently been allowed to be an exception to the rule.

Down in the dining-room the head waiter, sweating in his black coat and tie, showed me to a table that had no *reservada* notice on it. But just as I was about to look at the menu, the lights went out. I remembered the candle that stood in a saucer by my bedside, ready for just such an emergency that was, no doubt, not unusual, and then I went out to the balcony past the doors marked *Cavalheiros* and *Senhoras*.

Three Indians and three Europeans were sitting together at a table with their drinks. They were talking about the iron mines, which were developed in the fifties and are now the main prop of the Goanese economy. The Europeans were speaking English with a Germanic accent, and the conversation reminded me of the ore lighters I had seen from the plane, coming down the river past Vasco da Gama, the old port, to the modern port of Marmagoa.

The lights went on again, so I returned to the dining-room to find the waiters still standing at their stations along the side walls, looking like marionettes wound up ready to go into action. Glass pots that formerly contained the Japanese condiment Aji-no-moto, were being used for the pepper and salt. The head waiter bustled forward with the menu again.

"What would you like?" he said.

"Special Goa curry," I answered.

One of the marionettes jerked into motion and went off to the kitchen, returning presently with the curry and rice. In truth it was not bad, but there was nothing special about it. It was a simple fish curry, full of bones.

"Use the finger bowl, please," the marionette said.

I did as I was told, and then went out for a stroll in the cool of the evening. But it was not very cool. I could not understand why the Goanese, or indeed any of the Indians of the coastlands of the

South, where it is hot all the year round, go to the trouble of putting glass in their windows. Is it the desire for protection from the stinks and dust of the outside world, or for enclosing oneself inside one's house, that prevents them from adopting the Singapore system of open window spaces with iron grills across them for security?

On the Miramar alongside the Mandovi river all was quiet. There was hardly a car to be seen, although it was only nine, and soon the inevitable poor man attached himself to me. He was a young cleaner of cars, and he stood by patiently whilst I read the large sign outside the police barracks, which reproduced a quotation from the short lived prime minister, Lalbahadur Shastri, on his return from the Tashkent conference about defending peace with as much courage as was shown in resisting aggression. It meant nothing to him, as he spoke in Hindustani.

"This town is dead," he said. "It's like it was hit by a bomb. I am Hindu, but I say Portuguese time was better time for poor people. *Abhi bara danda hai. Sab chiz menga hogaya.* (Now there's a lot of hardship. Everything's become expensive.) Nobody come for *pini bini* (drinking and wenching) any more. Give me tea money, please. *Bhagwan* (God) bless you."

It certainly seemed dead, so I went in early, planning to start in good time the following morning. At the hotel desk there was another sign:

The Rotary Club of Panjim will celebrate World Understanding Week on March 12th. Understanding means Peace.

India seemed to be full of slogans and mottoes, as if to write them down and post them up in the magic English language were enough, without having to do anything to implement them.

Next morning I looked over the balcony at the river again. The sandy bank left by the tide looked inviting enough as the take-off point for a swim, but a man was squatting on it in full view, excreting, with his bare bottom turned towards me and his face gazing out to sea, willing unto himself the cloak of invisibility.

It was enough. I hired a car and went eight miles up river to leave the tawdry modern world behind and plunge into the strange peace of Old Goa. It was a pleasant drive through shady green plantations of coconuts and bananas. At the end of it, like a clearing in a forest, there was an open expanse of green lawns, bordered with low hedges of purple and white bougainvillea, and on either side of the

lawns stood the great cathedrals—to the right the dark red nave and
towers of the Bom Jesus, the colour of dried blood, and to the left
the white mass of Saint Catherine's.

I was fortunate in meeting Mr Alfred Braganza, the Goa corres-
pondent of All India Radio, who was lying in wait for the bishop in
the hopes of an interview. With him I went to look at the statue of
Camoens, which stands in the middle of the lawns, and was erected
as recently as 1960, only a year before Portuguese rule ended,
having been paid for by public subscription on the initiative of the
Lisbon newspaper, the *Diário Popular*. It might have been a symbol
of little Portugal, standing rigid and still on the seashore, calling out
like King Canute, whilst the tide of history rises ever higher.

Camoens wrote his epic of the sudden rise of the Portuguese
empire in the East in the middle of the sixteenth century, scarcely a
generation after Albuquerque had seized Goa and set it on its way
to becoming the capital city of the Viceroys of the Indies. He was a
soldier, and the cantos of the Lusiads vibrate with patriotic pride.
There is little mention of Goa in them, however, although the poet,
himself, spent six years of his life there, for the main part of the
poem is concerned with Vasco da Gama's first voyage to India and
his experiences in Calicut. But in the last canto the nymph Tethys
prophesies the exploits of da Gama's successors in India and the
conquests of Albuquerque. Richard Fanshaw's lively translation of
1655 goes well with the heroic theme:

> What glorious *Palms* do I see weaving *There*,
> With which his forehead VICTORY will crown,
> When without shadow or least touch of fear
> He shall win GOA's Isle of bright renown!
> But then (the *storm* obeying) will not bear
> So great a *Sayle*, and takes that *Bonet* down:
>   To reattempt the thing in fitter season.
>   FORTUNE and MARS fear *Valour* joyn'd with Reason.

> And (see) he does it; charges undismay'd
> Through *Walls*, through *Pykes*, through *Bullets*, and through *fire*:
> Opens the quilted *Squadrons* with his *Blade*
> Of MOORS and PAGANS knit in *Leagues* entire!
> His gallant *soldiers* in more blood shall wade
> Than *Lyons* pin'd, *Bulls* prickt with love and ire;
>   Upon the *Feast* (as pat as by designe)
>   Of EGYPT's *Virgin Martyr*, KATHERINE.

Half a century after the conquest the island had become very wealthy and was known as Golden Goa. Apart from the revenues coming in from the other Portuguese islands in the East, the trade in horses, which had been carried on in a small way by the previous inhabitants, was enormously increased to supply the flourishing empire of Vijayanagar up on the Deccan Plateau. Strangely enough horse-breeding was never a success in South India, probably for climatic and dietetic reasons, so fresh blood from Arabia and Persia was always in demand. This the Portuguese were able to supply from their bases in the Persian Gulf.

Meanwhile Saint Francis Xavier, the Apostle of the Indies, had come to Goa seeking the salvation of souls, and in 1554 his body was brought back from the China coast to lie in its silver casket in the church of Good Jesus to this day.

It was only by this church of Bom Jesus that there was any sign of life on the morning of my visit. People were going in through the doorway beside the College of the Jesuits, and we followed a group of pilgrims into the interior. Something like a blaze of sunlight met my eyes, and it then became easy to understand why Goa had been called "golden". The whole width and height of the church at the far end was taken up by a huge gilded reredos, with baroque columns behind the high altar. Between the columns stood a larger than life statue of Saint Ignatius Loyola. The altar itself was covered with a plain white tablecloth, as was the lower altar table, which was decorated with a frieze of the heads of the apostles.

The whole effect was a blinding vision of white and gold, which sent the Indian pilgrims into a passion of religious fervour. They moved from the main body of the church to the side chapel, where the body of Saint Francis lies, and kissed the silver reliquary containing the phalanx of one of the saint's thumbs, which is kept on the table in front of his mausoleum.

The mausoleum, itself, is in three parts. The lower platform is of jasper, the middle part, which raises the monument above man's height, is a chest of marble flanked with a scene from the life of the saint on each of its four sides. The upper part, which one must look up to, is the silver casket that actually contains the saint's body.

Saint Francis Xavier's life was really very short, for he was only forty-six when he died on Sancian Island off the coast of China. Of those forty-six years, his ministry in the East occupied less than eleven, since he was thirty-one before he was ordained a priest and thirty-six when he reached Goa. Briefly, the facts of his life are these. He went from his native Navarre in Spain to study at the University of Paris, and after he had gained his degree he taught there for a while. During part of this time Saint Ignatius Loyola was his room-mate. Together with five other companions they took vows of poverty and dedication to God's service. This was the origin of the Society of Jesus.

Saint Francis was then ordained in Venice, and from there he went to Rome. At his request, the Pope sent him to the Indies. With that fascinated link between love and fire, which was to come to grotesque fruition in the flames of the Inquisition, Saint Ignatius exhorted him to "go and set the whole world on fire with God's love".

In six years Saint Francis worked for the salvation of souls in Goa, on the Fishery coast of South India, in Ceylon, Malacca and the islands of Indonesia. Considering the great distances he covered, he could not have been on dry land more than five. Still his spirit took him even further. He went to evangelize Japan and spent two years there. Then he returned to Goa, but only to seek authority to try to evangelize China as well. Now he was Papal Nuncio in the East, and when the Governor of Malacca tried to stop him going any further, he excommunicated him. After his death his body was brought back to Malacca, where it remained in the church on the hill overlooking the strait that divides Malaya from Sumatra until it was returned to Goa.

In his life Saint Francis was said to have raised a girl from the dead in Madras, but it was in death that he was credited with working wonders. His body did not decompose, and during the time it lay at Malacca a pestilence that had been plaguing the town ceased. It remained incorrupt, and up till 1952 it was exposed for veneration once every ten years. It was then found to have become greatly dried up and shrivelled and was enclosed in a sealed glass coffin. In 1614 the right arm was amputated by Pope Paul V's decree and sent to Rome.

In 1964, on the occasion of the Pope's visit to the Eucharistic Congress in Bombay, the body was again exposed to view and seen to be still in a state of mummified preservation with quite recognizable features. So the people still come to the shrine in adoration and in the hope of help through life's toils and tribulations. As the prayer of Saint Francis Xavier says:

> My God, I love Thee, not because
>   I hope for heaven thereby;
> Nor because they, who love Thee not,
>   Must burn eternally,
> Not with the hope of gaining aught;
>   Not seeking a reward;
> But as Thyself hast loved me,
>   O ever-loving Lord.
> E'en so I love Thee, and will love,
>   And in Thy praise will sing;
> Solely because Thou art my God,
>   And my Eternal King.

The basilica of Bom Jesus was built in 1594 by the Jesuits, but the mausoleum was not finished till a hundred years later. However, the Jesuit convent, which is now lifeless, was finished only thirty-eight years after Saint Francis' death, and sent out missionaries all over the East from the seventeenth century onwards. A picture in a side room gave me some indication of what conversion to Christianity might have been like in those days. It showed a group of half-naked Indians bowing down to a priest, who was holding up a bloody crucifix. The conversion was simply from one ritual to another, and consequently the poor and uneducated formed the greatest number of converts, whilst very few upper class Hindus or Muslims were attracted to the faith.

Indeed, fear was as great an element in the conversion as love. And the fear became out of all proportion in the cathedral on the other side of the green lawns, for that was where the great bell tolled to announce the human sacrifice of the *auto da fé*.

The Cathedral of Saint Catherine was quite empty when we entered it through a side door. As in the Bom Jesus, a huge gilt complex of ornamentation covered the wall behind the high altar, whilst fourteen side altars were ranged along the walls. With their Corinthian columns and pediments they looked like miniature entrances to Classical temples, and each one contained gilded idols redolent of blood and suffering. In one Saint Catherine, herself, stood with six swords stuck into her chest, like a Tamil penitent at the feast of Thaipusam; in another the Christian warrior was shown with the cross on his shield; and in a third the Pope was receiving the keys of heaven from Saint Peter.

Though we found the great doors, that formerly opened on to the scenes of the inquisition, closed, religious services are still held in the cathedral from time to time. But the Convent of Saint Francis of Assisi, which is attached to it, is already almost a ruin. Doves were roosting in the roof and the floor was covered with their droppings. Yet their cooing did not seem to be out of place in a chapel dedicated to the gentle saint, who had actually preached sermons to the birds. What did seem strange was the juxtaposition of the convent next to a cathedral in which the main motif was blood and suffering and torture, both of the faithful martyrs and of the unfaithful free-thinkers.

The convent chapel was a large, high, simple building without the elaborate baroque statues, shrines and pillars of the cathedral and the basilica. The walls were painted with a repetitive floral pattern, giving the effect of wallpaper, predominantly green and cream in colour. Perhaps they were a reminiscence of its adaptation from a mosque, for this is the earliest of those buildings of Portuguese Goa that have not crumbled into ruin. The renovation of the Islamic shell was carried out only eleven years after the conquest, when the life of the colonizers was still simple, and the Inquisition had not yet been set up. High up in the roof I saw a wooden carving of Saint Francis, clinging to Christ crucified, with the motto, *Pobresa, Humilidade, Obediencia*—Poverty, humility, obedience.

In the cloisters of the convent there was an even stranger contrast, for they had been taken over by the Archaeological Survey of India for a museum, and were full of examples of the Hindu idols that had been anathema to the Christian friars. Phallic symbols in stone, many-armed goddesses with swelling breasts, dancing Sivas, elephant gods and monkey gods, and a strange torso of the twelfth century from Vetal, with a crab clinging to a hollow stomach and an elongated virile member hanging between the legs, were ranged along the flagstones that the friars once trod.

This invasion seemed to epitomize the returning tide of Hinduism, which I found a significant factor in many parts of India. But of course the Portuguese, zealous though they were, never actually eradicated the Hindus from their territories. The temples still survived in greater numbers than the churches, though with less magnificence, for the Hindus became second-class citizens.

Upstairs in the same convent the portraits of the first men of the first-class citizens had been hung up and stacked against the walls. The faces of viceroys, governors and generals, that had been removed

from the Idalcao palace in Panjim when the Indians took it over
from the Portuguese, stared out of the wood on which they had been
painted. In all the older ones there was a striking similarity—side-
whiskers, beards and moustaches, sharp, glistening eyes, prominent
noses, determined, jutting lips—the hallmarks of the conquerors. It
almost seemed as if one could trace the dying of the fire as the
generations passed, for the later ones had milder, softer faces, whilst
those of our own century, in white tie and black coat, looked quite
apologetic little men.

Mr Braganza and I left the convent and walked back past the
cathedral to the road running along the front of the cathedral
square. He was anxious not to miss the bishop, who was expected to
return to his quarters in the Convent of Saint Cajetan at about
midday. His anxiety turned into a slight panic when he discovered
that he had left his despatch case on the bus in which he had
travelled from Panjim.

But still the bishop did not arrive, and we went to look at the convent without him. It was empty except for a fierce dog, fortunately
chained, though it is still used as a seminary for ordained priests.
In the beautiful chapel, however, we found a humble Indian family
crossing themselves with consecrated water from a clam shell by the
door and adoring the cross on the low altar. In front of the high
altar an oil flame was burning blood red, enclosed in tinted glass, and
behind it stood the saint, surrounded by angels. Built on the lines of
Saint Peter's in Rome, it is a wonderful example of the Corinthian
style, white inside and out, though the central dome and some of the
walls are discoloured by moss.

Mr Braganza was calmed, in spite of the loss of his despatch case,
by our short visit to the chapel. "If God wills, I get my bag back,"
he said. "They are honest people. If not, I can't do anything about
it. Now I'll show you something else."

We walked towards the river, and came to an archway, through
which I could see a small jetty for a ferry and part of the island
opposite. It was not a large archway. You could have put it into the
Gateway of India in Bombay about ten times. Yet this had been the
Gateway of India for the Portuguese. It was through this Arch of
the Viceroys that every viceroy passed to enter the capital of
the Portuguese Indies, until the residence of the governor-general
was moved to Panjim in the middle of the eighteenth century.

It is an obvious reconstruction, built as recently as 1954, but the symbolic figures are still there—on the seaward side the Discoverer, Vasco, and on the landward side the Saint, spearing a supine Moor. Through the archway there was a scene that was like a small vignette of the old days. One of the heavy sailing barges of the region was ghosting down the river, and above it, on the green hill opposite, stood yet another of Goa's Catholic churches.

We turned away from the archway, and at that moment I thought we had looked at all there was to see, but Mr Braganza laughed. "You haven't seen half yet," he said. And forgetting his self-appointed rendezvous with the bishop, he took me back past the cathedral and the basilica, and up a shady pathway through some small plantations of mangoes, surrounded by stone walls.

"All this was Old Goa," he said. "All Velha Goa. There are ruins under all this land, and all these walls are made out of the ruins. What you've seen is only a small part. It stretches for acres and acres. There is a German woman I know digging now to see if she can find relics of the old days. All this was inhabited, until they could stay no more. There was too much fever and plague. But some said it was a punishment for the Inquisition, and the souls of the people burnt at the stake were having their revenge."

Walking up the small hill above the trees, we came upon a part of Old Goa that has not yet been reached by the restoration work carried out in this century with the active assistance of the Papal Nuncio. On either side grave, grey buildings stood bare and naked in the sun. The solid blocks of stonework of one convent stood alongside the five-tiered stone corner that was all that remained of another one, which had once belonged to the Augustinians. On the right side flying buttresses supported the wall of the Convent of Santa Monica, which was once deserted but has now been re-occupied, and is the only nunnery left in Old Goa.

A little further on we came to the forward edge of the hill, which overlooks the Mandovi river as it goes out to the sea. We found a small chapel there, blackened with age, which marks the spot where Afonso de Albuquerque stood victorious over the men of Bijapur at the reconquest of Goa on November 25th, 1510.

The Portuguese inscription refers to the "reconquest of Goa" because Albuquerque had already taken possession of Goa in February of the same year. At that time Cochin, the earliest European settlement in India, was the headquarters of the Portuguese, and when Albuquerque sailed north from there in January with

Goa—the martyrdom of Saint Catherine

Vijayanagar—*Yalli* on a deserted temple

Cochin—the fishing net

Cochin—in Communist Kerala

twenty-three ships, he announced that he was going to Ormuz to work on the fort there, and then going on to try to capture Aden.

He did neither. A Hindu pirate captain, whom he met on the island of Angediva, told him to go to Goa because the Moslem ruler was away and the Turks were building ships there to attack the Portuguese. That he was speaking as one pirate to another is evident from the way in which the Portuguese had just raided Calicut, burning and looting until they were driven off by the Nayars.

The fort at Panjim was taken without difficulty, and Goa was seized. But in three months time Yusuf Adil Shah, ruler of Bijapur, arrived with a large army, including many Turks, and forced the river which makes Goa an island. Albuquerque's attempt to enlist the aid of the Kings of Vijayanagar had been in vain, the inhabitants rose against him, and his captains wanted to get back to Cochin.

Albuquerque had the chiefs of Goa slain in revenge for the uprising of the people, and re-embarked. But the Portuguese could not leave. The constant wind of the south-west monsoon made it impossible for the ships to get out of the harbour and across the bar. Lying at the mouth of the harbour for three long months, they were at the mercy of artillery fire from the shore and subject to the hazard of fire-ships. The captains cursed Albuquerque for having delayed so long. The men suffered from hunger, thirst and sickness, and were near to mutiny.

He escaped in August, only to seek reinforcements to return to the attack. More ships had arrived from Portugal. Nevertheless their captains were reluctant to join him, as they were only interested in loading up with merchandise and returning home to cash in on their gains. So it was with the greatest difficulty that he managed to gather together 1,500 men to try again. This time his success was permanent. He reported back to the King of Portugal in the following words:

"In the capture of Goa Our Lord did much for us, since He willed that we should finish the great deed and do it better than we could have asked. More than 300 Turks perished there. Afterwards I burnt the city and put all to the sword, and for four days on end your men bled them. Wherever we could find them, no Moor was spared, and they filled the mosques with them and set them on fire. I ordered the cultivators and the Brahmins to be spared. We counted and found that 6,000 Moorish men and women had been slain.

7

"Sir, it was a great deed, well fought and well finished, and apart from Goa being so important, this is the first time revenge has been taken in India for the treachery and villainy your people have suffered from the Moors. Some Hindu chiefs, who had been robbed of their lands by the Turks, hearing of the destruction of Goa, came down from the mountains and helped me, and put to the sword all the Moors who escaped from the city.

"I shall not leave a single Moorish tomb or building standing, and the men taken alive I have roasted. I am handing over the property and lands of the Mosque to the Church of Saint Catherine, on whose day Our Lord gave us the victory on account of her virtue, and I am building this church in the large enclosure of the fort."

Thus the record shows that from the very beginning it was fire for human beings and love for God in Goa. For a hundred years and more the Portuguese prospered. Fortunes were made almost overnight, and soldiers who were shipped from Portugal, were granted one-way passages only. They were expected to pay for the return trip themselves, or not come back at all. Other Europeans called them derisively the "Fidalgos of Good Hope", because everyone added a "Dom" to his name, as if he were a member of the nobility, as soon as he entered the Indian ocean.

The Dutch came into the arena and cut off this prosperity. Tavernier, in the mid-seventeenth century, describes people who were rich on his first visit there, coming begging for alms the second time he called. Speaking of some of the women, he says they came to the door of the house in palankeens. "The visitor generally offers a letter from some religious person who recommends them, and speaks of the wealth she formerly possessed, and the poverty into which she has now fallen. Thus you generally enter into conversation with the fair one and in honour bound invite her to partake of refreshment, which lasts sometimes till the following day."

Tavernier also describes the Royal Hospital at Goa, which was the first hospital established by Europeans in the East and was renowned throughout India. It must have been somewhere near where we were standing, for it was at the western end of the town. Apart from the excessive bleeding usual in those days, patients were expected to undergo an unpleasant treatment borrowed from the Hindus. During the period of convalescence the prescribed medicine, to be taken three times a day for twelve days, was the urine of cows.

Of all the secular and religious activity of the centuries only the religious side remains. The fires have burnt down and gone out, but the love has survived. The Jesuit schools and colleges remain firmly established all over India, welcomed for the devotion of the teachers to the children they educate.

As we stood beside the barred door of the chapel of Saint Catherine, a group of nuns of all nations from the Convent of Santa Monica came along the pathway, formed a circle in the shade of the building and began to sing. They were dressed in pure white, and their English song came sweet and clear through the warm tropical air.

Mr Braganza had by now given up all thought of waylaying the bishop, and suggested we should return to the café by the basilica for a drink. On the way we, ourselves, were waylaid. A middle-aged man came bustling up to us and recounted his story.

He said that he, himself, had been a government servant, and his brothers were professional men and important men of business. But he had suffered from epileptic fits, and no doctor had been able to effect a cure. He had had to give up his job and live in misery and in fear of the fits. Then he had turned to Saint Francis Xavier and been cured. He handed me a little printed card out of a brief-case, with a picture of the Saint in dark blue, standing under a palm-tree holding up a cross, and dark, half-naked men looking up to him in awe. And on the reverse side the dedication was written: "At the feet of the Glorious Apostle of the Indies, S. Francisco Xavier, on the sixth day of his Novena of Thanks, in the spirit of gratitude for favours received." Then came his name and the date, which was that very day.

"A Xavier *bhakti*," I said.

Mr Braganza looked mystified.

"I mean, they talk about Siva *bhakti* and Vishnu *bhakti* as devotees of Siva and Vishnu, so he is a Xavier *bhakti* as a devotee of Saint Francis."

He laughed. "Yes. True, true," he said. "A Xavier *bhakti* he is."

6

SIVA'S NIGHT

I CAUGHT the express bus for Vijayanagar at the bus stand opposite the post office in Panjim. It sounds an easy move, but the journey was not so simple, for the bus was only due to go as far as Hubli, which was enough after the long climb up the Ghats. From there I would have to catch a train, which would drop me at Hospet at four in the morning, and from Hospet there were another nine miles to cover, by means unknown, to reach the remains of the city whose trade in horses made Goa rich. The 1962 edition of the guide book referred to pony *jhatkas,* which would be obtained by the stationmaster, but I trusted that, as in many other sections, it would prove to be behind the times.

The bus was only a third full, so that all my efforts to find the office of the Mysore State Transport Company on the previous day and make a booking had been needless. The young man in the upper storey room between the registrar's office and the labour exchange had been right to tell me not to worry. As nobody, apparently, went by train either, and the hotel clerk could not even tell me its departure time, even though there was only one a day, it seemed that not many travellers were in the habit of going up on to the Deccan.

Of the few who were on the move I noticed in particular a young German, wearing a pseudo-Indian dress, consisting of a long, white nightshirt over a pair of cotton trousers and, on his head, a purple handkerchief, armed with books on spiritual meditation and yoga. But my seat companion was an Indian government accountant, who had been posted from Nagpur to Goa, as he said, "under pressure" soon after the takeover. He was now going to his home near Hospet on leave, before taking up another appointment in his own locality.

We settled down to our seven-hour journey. The driver was in khaki, like so many government servants in India, whether they are concerned with the army or not, and he was wearing military style metal shoulder titles with the letters M.S.T. on them. On the other hand the conductor was in nondescript civilian clothes, and spent an interminable time fiddling over the small change for the price of the tickets, which had been calculated at an awkward fraction instead of being rounded off to the nearest rupee.

Though Goa looks tiny enough on the map of India, it took us two and three-quarter hours to reach the border of the New Conquests, travelling at a fair speed, with only two stops, one to pick up some crates of coca-cola, and one to relieve ourselves. We swept through Old Goa, where I had spent so much time, then wound our way through Ponda and out on to the paddy fields, getting ever closer to the line of hills.

The border is 2,000 feet up in the jungle at the top, but the customs officials do not go that far. They keep watch down below. After passing the customs post the road began to climb seriously, winding its way up through the trees. Distances were now marked on the roadside in kilometres, but I noticed that the heights remained in feet. There were cosy signs, written in English, at frequent, repetitive intervals, such as, "Ghat road. Please drive slowly", and "Narrow/Bends. Drive slowly".

Traffic was non-existent and, in spite of the signs, the bus was driven as fast as it would go. But the road was too steep for it to reach a dangerous speed, and the driver had to wait until we had slipped over the rim of the plateau before he was able to roar and rattle ahead, and make it live up to its name of an express. We passed through deep forest country, where lemurs were to be seen prancing about amongst the trees, and the lumberjacks' lorries hogged the road until our frantic blasts on the horn made them pull to the side.

Just short of Londa, where we made our first stop in Mysore state, the road forking off to Belgaum reminded me of the time I had gone down there from Poona during the war to look for tiger in these same forests. It was six o'clock, the hour of dusk, and the cool of the Deccan sundown, with the bullock carts and the straw and the tangy smell of the dust, brought another place back out of the recesses of my mind—Mhow in the province of Central India, now called Madhya Pradesh, where I had trained as a cadet in the Indian Army.

We went on into the dusk, and just before darkness closed in we passed a large sign on the left of the road. The accountant turned to me with a look of satisfaction on his face.

"This is Kittur," he said. "That sign tells about the Rani of Kittur, who led the first war of independence."

"Against whom?" I asked.

"Against the British, of course. It was in 1824. There was a fort here until the British destroyed it in revenge."

"Oh yes," I said. "I think I remember. There was some kind of local revolt. People thought the Company was done for because the Sepoys had mutinied at Barrackpore. They didn't want to go and fight in Burma. Some officers were killed and so was the collector. He was an uncle of Thackeray, the writer."

"She was a glorious lady," the accountant said.

"And when was the second war of independence?"

"That was 1857."

"Ah, the Indian Mutiny."

"That one was nearly successful."

"But I saw the sign was in English all the same."

"Of course. The war was against the English."

"So that's why it's in English?"

"Naturally."

I opened my mouth to say something else, but at that moment the bus stopped. The road was blocked by an army recovery vehicle, which was craning up a lorry that had fallen into the ditch at the side of the road. There was a good deal of hubbub and shouting, and pulling and pushing, watched by a mixed group of spectators from the local village and the halted traffic.

The lorry was hanging dangerously at an angle, held up by its flimsy superstructure. There was more shouting. The sergeant looked up. He looked at me. Was it imagination, or was it merely a reaction from past years? The look seemed to say that, if I would take charge, he would willingly hand over the responsibility. I almost stepped forward automatically, but then I remembered just in time. I was nothing to do with it. I was only one of the spectators. Eventually the lorry fell upright on the road, and the superstructure was wrenched into some semblance of shape to let us pass. I went back to my place in the bus beside the accountant.

We stopped next at Dharwar, which grew to importance as the headquarters of the Southern Mahratta railway. Then we continued another thirteen kilometres to the bus station at Hubli. It was the end of the ride, but there was no respite. Men and boys were shouting at us, first through the windows of the bus and then face to face after we had alighted. I only had a light bag, and all I wanted was to hire a porter and walk the mile to the station, possibly stopping to eat something on the way. This is what I thought I had managed to do, until I found my bag stuffed in with a lot of other luggage belonging to the accountant on a two-wheeled pony trap—a *tikka gari* or *tonga*, as they are called.

There was argument over the fare, and I offered to take my bag off and go my own way, but this was not acceptable. Having got two travellers, the tonga wallah was not prepared to let one go. So we set off, with the lean pony straining at the overladen trap.

We had been going five minutes, when the accountant, who had been counting up his baggage as though he were casting a column of figures, suddenly called out to the tonga wallah to stop. He had left a suitcase behind.

"So many," he explained. "Moving all my house and baggages, you see. Please wait."

He rushed off back to the bus station. The tonga wallah grumbled. The pony farted. I thought again of removing my own bag and going on alone, but it seemed that I was committed. The accountant returned to load yet another piece on to the tonga, and we set off again.

At the station we parted. As soon as he had run into a friend of his, the accountant did not seem to care much for knowing me any more, so I walked into the station on my own to get my ticket and wait in the lugubrious waiting room. No food was to be had but packets of biscuits, and the only signs of animation to be seen were in two officers of the Sikh regiment, a captain and a lieutenant, who left shortly after I entered.

The train left shortly after 11 p.m.—a slow train called a Passenger to distinguish it from the Mail train and the Express. A thick film of dust covered the berths and the floor of the compartment, which I found I had got to myself, so clearing a clean space on which to lie down was the first task. The next was sleep. But sleep did not come easily as we clattered along the uneven track. Furthermore it was no ordinary night. It was *Sivaratri*, the Night of Siva, and the fields on either side of the track were full of blazing fires for the people keeping the night-long vigil.

According to the legend the vigil of Sivaratri originated in an accidental vigil kept by a hunter, who became thereby an animal lover and a saint. He had been arrested for debt and confined in a Siva temple. In the evening he was released by a devotee, a Siva *bhakti*, who paid off the debt on his behalf. He went straight to the forest to look for game, and hid himself in the foliage of a bel tree, the leaves of which are sacred to Siva.

The hunter repeated the name of Siva to himself, which he had heard in the temple, although he did not know what it meant. He also happened to shake down some leaves of the bel tree onto a stone phallus, the emblem of Siva, that was standing on the ground below. At nightfall a doe approached, and he drew his bow. The doe was pregnant, and promised that, if he spared her to give birth to her young, she would return to be killed. She said that there was another doe following her, who had been a dancer, but she had neglected to dance before Siva, and as a punishment she had been turned into a doe and mated with an *asura*, who had been turned into a black buck.

The hunter's feelings towards animals had already been partly softened by repeating the name of Siva. So he let the pregnant doe go. Presently the second doe came along, seeking her mate, and he spared her too. Then the black buck appeared, and in spite of his hunger and frustration, the hunter let him go too.

The first doe went home and delivered her young, and the black buck and the second doe found conjugal bliss. In gratitude each one of them vied with the others to be the one to offer its life to the hunter. Meanwhile, however, the hunter's sins had been expiated by his vigil and by the repetition of Siva's name. He realized it was evil to kill living creatures for meat, preached a sermon to all three of them, and let them go. Thereupon he was translated into Siva's heaven in a celestial car.

It is a gentle legend to be connected with Siva, for Siva's devotees maintain that he is the same as Rudra, the Vedic god of storms, and most of his attributes seem to derive from Murugan, a demoniac fertility god of the dark Tamils of the non-Aryan South. He is the world in flux, the dynamic god of destruction and reproduction. His dance represents the motion of the universe. He wears a tiger skin, and snakes are coiled in his matted hair. He haunts cremation grounds, carrying a skull in one hand and a begging bowl in the other. His weapon is the trident and his symbol the phallus.

I slept little, thinking of the hold Siva has over millions of India's peasants, who are never far from the destruction of famine and ever caught in the process of reproduction. When I did sleep, I woke again with a start, thinking I had gone on beyond my station. It was 3.45. On the horizon, beyond the fires dotted in the fields, a long line of lights blazed. They marked the site of the great new dam across the Tungabhadra river, which is one of the many projects going ahead with foreign aid in the battle to feed the ever rising population. I wondered pessimistically who would have the last laugh—Siva or the technological planners.

A quarter of an hour later the ancient engine hissed and steamed to a halt at Hospet. I got out and walked into the hall of the station, in which nearly all the space was taken up by rows of bodies lying wrapped in their dirty white cloths. As in the side streets of Bombay, they were not corpses in their shrouds, as they appeared to be, but living beings. I would have sought a retiring room, in which to rest, but again there was no respite. There was a clamour of voices, and someone seized my bag and made off with it. Of course I had no option but to follow. There, in the station yard, were the low carts with hoods over them, like miniature two-wheeled covered wagons, called *jhatkas,* to which the guide book referred. Mine did not even have a pony. It was pulled by a donkey, and the only way one could sit in it was cross-legged.

I quailed at the thought of having to cover nine miles in this vehicle. But things were not quite as bad as they appeared to be. We were to go only a mile or so to the bus station and proceed from there. I would have preferred to walk, yet each time I made motions to get out, the *jhatka* wallah whipped up his wretched beast, thinking I was dissatisfied with our speed.

We stopped beside a little ornamental circle containing a recently moulded bust of the Chairman of the Municipal Board. In the dim light he looked most life-like and benign.

"Very good man," the *jhatka* wallah said.

We walked over to the tea house, where I sat down and ordered coffee. The char wallah dexterously mixed the coffee and milk together, shooting it from glass to glass at a distance of two or three feet, and handed it to me. It was excellent. I was pleased to find something in India at last that was as good as anywhere else. Meanwhile the *jhatka* wallah hung around with a few other night birds chatting. After all, now that the train had arrived and he had been the lucky one to get a fare, there was nothing else to do.

At a quarter to five the bus arrived and disgorged a mass of people, who were returning from the Sivaratri vigil at Vijayanagar. After they had cleared out, I took my place. At five we tried to start, but the battery was flat and a push was needed. Passengers were not inclined to get out, so it was fortunate that a man and a boy were able, between them, to rock the bus enough to spark the engine off.

Our destination was Hampi, the village that lies in the middle of the old ruins of Vijayanagar. We drove in darkness along a bumpy country road with cactus hedges that loomed up in strange shapes as we passed them. Then came a sharp bend, and even stranger, the dim outlines of the columns and roof of a building that looked as though it might have come from ancient Greece. Then we rolled down a short hill and came to a stop.

The bus was immediately attacked by a great crowd of peasant people, wrapped in their white cloths, who wanted to get on. It was just not possible, since we, who were already on, wanted to get off. Yet there was no order of any kind. We had to fight to get out of the bus, and those outside who had fought hardest to get closest, were the first to squeeze themselves on. One clever fellow tried to get in through the window, but got stuck half-way, suspended in the air, until he was helped down.

I looked up. And a sight of pagan grandeur met my eyes. Quite close, at the end of a straight road that was crowded with the shadowy figures of men and women, a great tower, bathed in orange light, soared high up against the blue-black background of the night sky. It was the gateway to the Siva temple, which returned to life after the rest of Vijayanagar had died, and is now a thriving centre of pilgrimage.

In the pagodas of South India, unlike those of the Orissan style, it is the gateways, called *gopurams,* that rise to great heights, whilst the temples inside the walls are relatively low buildings. This *gopuram,* 165 feet high and covered all over with plaster images of men, women and beasts, made the actual entrance doorway look quite diminutive. After I had passed the stalls of those who sell the red and purple sandalwood for the Sivaite signs plastered on the forehead, and of the traders in glass bangles, sweets and toys, and after I had run the gauntlet of the two rows of beggars, blowing their conches and beating their begging tins, I was amazed to find how large and massive the entrance actually is.

I entered the first courtyard, and put my bag in a room which, to my surprise, had been set aside for left luggage at a small charge of twenty-five paisa per person. The crowd was vast, yet nobody had made use of it. The pilgrims travel light, and keep all they need in a small bundle attached to their clothing, so I had no need to fear that the absence of any kind of baggage check would make it difficult for me to find my own case again.

In the big courtyard the people were sitting about in family and village groups. Some were drumming and singing, others silent, their vigil nearly ended. Dawn came up. The garish lights and the fires of the pilgrims faded, and the magic paled with them.

I looked at the doorway to the inner shrine, and thought that it would be forbidden to me. But one of the temple staff, with a blue and red cloth draped across his shoulder as a badge of office, came bustling up to me, eager to take me in. He had been a *saddhu* for eight years, he said, though previously he had been a government inspector of co-operatives.

This was indeed a change from the past, and I wondered whether the pained controversy in recent years as to whether non-Hindus should be allowed inside the inner sanctuaries of Hindu temples had something to do with it, for many Indians now oppose those temple authorities that exclude the stranger to their religion. They bewail the bigotism and intolerance that survives in the land where the Buddha and Mahatma Gandhi were born. They contrast the secretive Hindu temples with the open Christian churches.

To be fair, there was a good deal of excuse for secretiveness in the past, for Muslims commonly came to destroy, and Christians, as often as not, came as though they were witnessing abominations and went home to mock. But now that India is independent there is a different spirit abroad, and many feel that anyone who approaches in due decency and seriousness should be allowed in. Each temple decides for itself, since there is no organized Hindu church to speak as one voice, and the High Priest of Puri still sets his heart against the stranger at the gate.

It may be suggested that, for some, there is a deeper reason for keeping up the veil. Many of the temple authorities, if persuaded to answer in all honesty, would have to confess that the idols and totems, which they surround with elaborate show, are indeed ridiculously unworthy of any thoughtful mind, and are used mainly to impress the simple peasant people, if not to bamboozle them.

They are like men who are unwilling to admit that the play is over and come out into the world of reality.

The ex-government inspector took me in to see the shrine of Virupaksha, which is Siva's guise in this particular place. He pointed out every little idol in its own shrine, the more important of them in low, dark rooms, placed in such positions that one would have to bow or kneel to see them properly. The people moved about haphazardly, for there was no fixed time to attend, no temple communion like a church service. There was nothing striking about any of the figures, and I was glad to get outside again and climb the mound that rises on the south side of the temple wall.

A jumble of stony hills met my eyes, with the river winding over a rocky bed between them on the other side of the temple. I knew that the ruins of Vijayanagar, the "City of Victory", were stretched around me, but it was difficult to tell which was ruin and which was merely a natural hill of piled-up boulders. There was no obvious area of concentration or outstanding building, except for the nearby temple.

Yet in its heyday less than 500 years ago Vijayanagar was a large city twenty-four miles round, with half a million inhabitants. It was founded at a time when the Turkish Sultans ruled in Delhi and the Sword of Islam had penetrated right down to Madurai in the far south. In the course of one of its campaigns the Sultan's army took prisoner a Hindu chief named Harihara. He was converted to Islam, and then sent back to the south to restore the Sultan's authority over the Bahmani kingdom, which was also Mohammedan. Harihara did this, but then reverted to Hinduism and declared his independence. He was readmitted to caste status and affirmed to be the earthly representative of the local deity, Virupaksha.

Vijayanagar was built, and became the capital of the kingdom of the same name in 1343. It stretched from coast to coast across southern India and remained a permanent bastion against the Sultans to the north for over 200 years. Goa was taken and became its window on the world across the sea. The port was lost eventually to the Sultan of Bijapur, so that when it fell, in turn, to the Portuguese, Vijayanagar had a strong motive for establishing friendly relations with the newcomers.

At that time Krishnadeva Raya was on the throne. Portuguese travellers were impressed by the wealth and splendour of his court, and Paez called him "the most feared and perfect king that could possibly be". In his statue he looks like one of the sun gods of Konarak. He built up his cavalry with the horses the Portuguese sent him.

But in the end it was to no avail. Four of the Sultanates into which the Bahmani kingdom had broken up—Bijapur, Golconda, Ahmednagar and Bidar—united to mount a concerted attack. It was the year 1564. The Raja of Vijayanagar marched north to meet the Muslims on the other side of the Kistna river at a remote spot called Talikota well over 100 miles away. The citizens of his capital were not too worried. These attacks had occurred many times before. But this time something went wrong. At first the Hindus had the advantage, but then skilful handling of the Mohammedan cavalry and artillery turned the tide. The Raja was captured and executed, and the rout began. Subsequently Vijayanagar was sacked—reduced in one day from a prosperous city to a ruin.

Now only a few of the stone buildings remain, the thousands of mud houses having long ago sunk back into the soil. The elephant stables and the baths can be seen, together with a huge elephant headed man and another with a lion's head, a chariot in stone, and besides the great pagoda, some other temples with the curious monsters called the *yalli* carved on them, biting their own tails.

I went over the brow of the mound past some small stone buildings, which showed evidence of fine construction and former elegance, and came upon a row of half a dozen women excreting in familiar chatty company, with their bare bottoms towards me. It was enough to turn me back to the main road, for now I saw that many groups of the Siva vigilantes were walking purposefully towards the periphery of the temple in all directions. There were clearly no sanitary arrangements of any kind. Yet the sun was already up. The best that each group could do was to seek its pitch and pretend that it was invisible to the others.

I walked down the main road, which is the one the wooden chariot follows when the god takes his outing during the Jatra festival, to the huge stone bull at the other end of it. Then I climbed the paved path over a low hill to one of the empty temples. The lion defeating the elephant was a constant motif, as at Konarak. "D.D.T. treated 28.8.59" a notice said. Squirrels ran in and out of the empty halls, and monkeys, perched on the tops of the big, round boulders, looked down. They were happier than the men, who were hacking away at the old roots of scrub bushes for a little fuel in land that was already denuded and bare.

Now the Siva devotees were making their way down to the river bank and through a narrow cut in the rocks to the bathing place. I followed them a little way, but the dirt-caked saddhus in their leopard skins, and the shouting beggars were too much for my resolve, and I turned away.

Back in Hampi crowds were making a wild rush for each bus as it arrived on its return from Hospet. I went towards the restaurant to get something to drink whilst waiting for the crowd to thin out. But it was called a Brahmin establishment, and I sheered away, afraid to risk the indignity of being thrown out by the people who were sitting up there on the stone terrace looking down at me. It was better to buy some oranges and bananas and wait in the shade of the building that reminded me of Greece.

A round-faced, whiskered farmer spoke to me and offered me a guava.

"Where are you from?" I said.

"From Devahalli," he answered in Hindi. "I come here every year for Sivaratri, and for the Jatra."

"What is the harvest like this year?"

"Good."

"Enough food?"

"Plenty."

"Not like in Bihar."

"Bihar? I don't know about Bihar. That's a long way. Why don't you eat that guava?"

"I don't want one now," I said. "I've just finished some bananas and an orange."

"Where are you going?"

"To Hospet."

"You must push to get on the bus. Push hard."

"You push. I'll follow."

"Look. Here's one coming now. This way. Quick."

We moved forward, but the rest of the crowd was quicker. After a brief struggle we returned defeated to the Greek pavilion.

"You didn't push hard enough," the farmer said. "I told you to push hard."

"I was following you," I said.

"No good following me. I'm waiting here till the others have gone."

Having eaten little since lunch-time the previous day, I was getting hungry, and when the next bus came, hunger gave me the impetus to push hard enough to squeeze myself in. The route back was a different one, past a large artificial lake beside the village of Kamalpur, with a retaining bund that had been modernized from the earthen wall that already existed in the old days of Vijayanagar's fame. Near the village acres of thriving green rice and vegetables showed what a difference the life-giving water makes. A convoy of bullock carts, drawn by the long-horned Mysore cattle with brass caps on their horns, wallowed in and out of the ruts in the road.

By the time I reached the station, after another *jhatka* ride, my hunger had grown sharper still, so I walked into the station dining-room. Inside, each diner was sitting at a separate little square table, with his left arm standing vertically up in the air, balanced on his elbow, which rested on the table. With his right hand he kneaded and mixed food together from circular aluminium trays and popped it into his mouth.

I sat down at my separate table, which was only just big enough for me to get my knees under it. Eyes turned towards me. I wondered what to do next. Was it self-service, perhaps? No. There was a waiter bringing trays to the tables. Then what? Of course, I must wash my hands. Since I was going to eat with my hands, they were expecting me to wash my hands. It did not matter that I had already washed them in the waiting-room. I went to the tap in the corner of the room, held my fingers under the running water for a few seconds, then returned to my table.

The eyes at the other tables went back to their own trays. The waiter came to me. "Rice or bread?" he asked.

"Bread."

"How many?"

"Four."

He went out to the kitchen, and returned almost immediately with a large aluminium tray and an aluminium bowl. On one side of the tray there were four round, flat, grey cakes of unleavened bread of the kind we used to call *chapatis* in northern India. On the other side there was a large dollop of vegetables in a yellow curry, a smaller dollop of oily fried vegetables, a little pile of rough salt, and another little pile of mixed ground spices. In the round bowl there was a white yoghourt.

Thinking that I knew well enough what to do, I broke bread and scooped at the dollop of curry with a piece of chapati. Then I ate

the curry without smearing too much of it in my hand. I tried again
with the other, smaller dollop. I licked my oily fingers, then looked
up, congratulating myself on not having done too badly.

The eyes at the separate tables were looking at me, and the hands
on the ends of the vertical arms, which had been flapping up and
down in loose gestures as one man talked to another, were still.
Eyes looked at other eyes, communicating a half-hidden, super-
cilious contempt, near to open laughter.

Then it dawned on me. Being left-handed, I had automatically
used the left hand. I had broken bread with both hands, mixed
food with the left hand, put it into my mouth with the left hand, and
actually licked the fingers of the left hand. And the left hand is the
unclean hand, the hand that rinses the bottom with the water from
the little brass pot, the hand that flaps about at the end of the
vertical arm, that gesticulates and gyrates, but never touches the
food. "What can you expect of an outcaste, of a *mlechchha*?"
the eyes seemed to say. "We know quite well they are unclean.
This only proves what we already know."

I brought the right hand into use as inconspicuously as possible,
but the problem was how to tear off pieces of chapati with only one
hand. It needed a good deal of dexterity with the fingers, and how,
the eyes seemed to say, could a *mlechchha* be expected to be dexter-
ous with his fingers? One had to anchor the chapati with three
fingers, then tear the pieces off with the fourth finger and thumb.
Then one had to be forthright and plunge the fingers right into the
mess of curry. There was no need to be finicky, for this was the
right hand, the clean hand. This was all right. Other diners, I saw,
had it covered with oil and grease up to the wrist.

There still remained one more problem to be solved, and that was
how to eat the yoghourt. It was too stiff and solid to upend the bowl
to the mouth and drink. On the other hand it was not solid enough
to pick up pieces with the fingers. The problem seemed so intract-
able that I was prepared to leave the yoghourt altogether, but then the
solution was provided by a young man with sleek, glossy hair three
separate tables away. He was not a bread eater, he was a rice eater,
and he had been rolling his rice in his curry into a fine mess and
squashing it into his mouth with sucking, gurgling noises. His whole
hand was covered with rice grains and oil and salt and curry, but it
was quite clean, because it was the right hand. Finally he inserted
the index finger of his clean hand into the yoghourt and twirled it

around. This turned it from a junket into a porridge, which he poured slowly down his throat.

I went to the corner again and washed my hands.

"More?" the waiter asked.

"No, thank you."

"One rupee."

Thinking it was quite a good meal for a rupee, I paid up willingly. Then I left the dining-room and went along to the ticket-office.

"I want a first class ticket to Bangalore," I said.

"Are you having reservation?"

"Not yet. May I make a reservation, please."

"It is not possible to make reservation now."

"Then I'll take the ticket and hope for the best."

"You cannot have ticket unless you have reservation."

"But you said I cannot have a reservation."

"Exactly. It is too late to make reservation."

"So I can't have a ticket."

"Not to say cannot have ticket."

"But you said I couldn't have a ticket without a reservation."

"That is so."

"There's no room in the first class, then."

"Not to say, there is no room. There will be room."

"Then I'd like a ticket, please."

"I cannot give you a ticket. First wait till the train comes. Then there will be making reservation."

"You can't tell me yet whether I will get a berth?"

"You will get a berth."

"But you cannot sell me a ticket yet?"

"Exactly. Having no reservation."

"There will be time to get a ticket after the train has arrived?"

"Plenty of time. Don't worry. Don't worry."

The stationmaster—the man who, according to the guide book, "will arrange for a pony jhatka"—was right. There was plenty of time. But first there was more time to wait, and I was lucky enough, at that moment, to meet two young men of the United States Peace Corps to while the time away. They were on their way back to the nearby village where they were living and working.

At that time there were 800 members of the Peace Corps in India, living with middle class Indians, using the same kind of accommodation, and eating with them as far as the limitations of caste

8

restrictions would allow. They were concerning themselves with education, agriculture, hygiene and other aspects of improvement of the standard of living of the people, and their number was soon to be increased to 1,500.

They were thus heirs to a noble tradition of service, in the line of that small band of selfless Europeans, who for generations have thrown their lives into the sea of poverty, ineptitude, dirt and despair of the Indian multitudes, and tried to improve conditions by practical example. I wondered how many of them had heard of the great work of Brigadier Brayne in rural uplift, who, in the words of an Indian state premier, "by dint of perseverance and practical sympathy almost single-handed set up a new tradition in the rural Punjab."

That was before the massacres and the mass migrations tore the Punjab apart. But, in any case, the work is never ending. The sea is too vast, and the guiding lighthouses are always far too few. I asked one of the young men what his main preoccupation was, and I was not surprised to find it was the same one that has plagued India for generations.

"I try to get the landlords to take some kind of an interest in their land," he said. "I tell them that where I come from, if a man's got land, he's always out on it seeing to things and keeping things on the line. He's right out there every day. Some of these people, if they're out there once a month, they think they're doing just fine."

He said they were working on getting the farmers interested in better strains of crops, and on the right kinds of cultivation for the new lands to be irrigated by the Tungabhadra dam. It seemed a great task for two young men, working with no authority and simply trying to persuade by means of demonstration and example.

"When we get really stewed up, we go down to Bangalore and cool off in the Three Aces bar," he said. "It's air-conditioned."

The Peace Corps boys got into the second-class, and I climbed into the first-class compartment to which a station official had tied my reservation tag, then rushed off back down the platform to get my ticket. I had it to myself until we reached Bellary. There I was joined by a shy young geologist, who told me he was living out in the forest sixty kilometres away, proving a seam of iron ore.

"What about the famous diamonds of Golconda?" I said.

"There are none left," he answered. "But there is one place in Rajasthan where they are finding diamonds now."

Thirty miles further on, at Guntakal junction, two more people joined us, making the numbers in our four-berth compartment complete. One of them was a thick-set dark man, who was an inspector of police, and the other was a salesman from Bombay, who explained that he was travelling by rail because his car had a broken radiator hosepipe. It seemed to me to be a small matter to have interfered with his whole mode of travel.

The inspector, on whom the mantle of the sahibs had fallen, was travelling in the traditional manner of the sahibs, with a bedding roll, wrapped in a canvas cover with leather straps, and a large felt-covered water bottle. But the salesman simply produced a red sheet out of his suitcase and spread it over his berth.

"I travel light," he said. "No bother with coolies."

"What is all that, then?" the inspector said, pointing at six large boxes, which filled all the spare space in the compartment.

"That is exceptional. That is stationery."

"Is it permit forms you are having?"

"Not to say permit forms. That is order forms."

"What are you ordering?"

"I am not ordering. I am selling. Cigarettes I am selling."

"Very good. It is lucky thing the hosepipe on your car broke."

"Why do you say lucky? I am thinking very unlucky thing."

"That stationery. You never get it in your car. It is too heavy. Why are you not buying the stationery in Bangalore?"

"This is special stationery. Office notepaper. Order forms. I am opening one office in Bangalore."

"Very good. So you stay in Bangalore?"

"First I am staying, then going back to Bombay."

"You are leaving one man in Bangalore?"

"No. I am number one man in Bangalore, but I am thinking I am going back to Bombay for my car."

"When they have finished mending the hosepipe."

"Exactly. They are having much difficulty. It is the size of the hosepipe. It is an unusual size."

"Can they import one?"

"No permit."

"Then they must manufacture one. The mechanics in Bombay are very good. They will manufacture one."

"They are trying. Little by little they are trying."

"Very good. So how many cigarettes are you selling?"

"My factory makes two crores, fifty lakhs cigarettes a day. The tobacco comes from Andhra Pradesh, what they used to call Hyderabad."

"That must be twenty-five million," I said.

"Very good," the inspector said. "That is not enough."

"It is a lot," the salesman said.

"But still, it is not enough. There are four hundred million Indians. Say half of those are women, who are not smoking. That leaves two hundred million. Fifteen per cent children and fifteen per cent aged. That is less sixty million, leaving one hundred and forty million. That is only one cigarette for six or seven people. It is not enough."

"There are other factories as well. And we are not making the cheap *biris*. They are reserved for the cottage industries. So we are making enough with the other factories and without the biris."

"You say the population is four hundred million," I said to the inspector. "I think you are a bit behind the times. The officials say it is over five hundred million now."

"Then if they are saying that, perhaps they are right. I am learning all these figures at school."

"But it certainly was only four hundred million ten years ago."

"So we are all the time making plenty of children!"

"Don't you think it's time to stop?"

"Stop! We cannot stop, man! You are not thinking. This is a hot country. The people will never stop."

"But some kind of birth control?"

"What is this birth control? No. Only control we are having is nature control."

"But think. How are you going to feed all these extra people?"

"We are making arrangements. We are building dams, you see, and watering more land and growing more food. There is plenty of land. All we have to do is bring the water to it. Don't you worry, man! And then there is wars. We should be grateful to China and Pakistan for helping with the birth control."

"But think. Even now there are shortages of food. In Kerala and Andhra Pradesh and Mysore there is a shortage of food. And Madras has sealed off her borders to stop her food being taken away into the deficit areas."

"I know. I know very well," the inspector said. "And we are having extra check posts and also having armed pickets patrolling the border. But that is not food shortage. That is control of the food. We have to stop the criminal classes smuggling the food."

"There are many criminals?"

"Of course there are criminals. If there were no criminals, there would be no need of government."

"I thought it was because of food shortage that they wanted to smuggle the food."

The inspector would not be drawn. "They are criminal classes," he insisted. "I am saying there must be control on the criminal classes, but there is no food shortage."

"But what about Bihar? According to reports there is actual famine in Bihar now."

"Bihar is a long way."

"I know. But it's part of India."

"I think you are being mistaken. I am not hearing any reports of famine in Bihar."

"I read about it in the English newspapers."

"Ah, it is some trick then. There are some persons wanting to discredit our government for their own ends. If there was food shortage in Bihar, government would be telling that."

"I was in a food shortage in Bengal in 1943," I said. "There were two million dead by the time it was over."

"That was British time," the inspector said. "Now we are independent country, there cannot be food shortage."

"But what about the food America sends to India. Isn't that because of food shortage?"

"They must send. Otherwise the food will rot. We are not forcing them to send. All this sending from other countries, we are not wanting that. We can do everything for ourselves. We are having the rice, the coconuts, tea, coffee, sugar, everything. Why do we want foreign aid? We are independent peoples."

"Even when people are dying of famine?"

"If there is food shortage, and people are dying, that is nature. Those people can be proud to die. My god, man! They are martyrs. They are martyrs for independence." He belched, and the rice he had eaten at Guntakal rumbled in his belly. "I am telling you," he said, "those people who are telling you there is food shortages in Bihar are criminal classes. They are only wanting to stir up trouble for their own ends."

The geologist had kept silent during this talk, and made no

comment now. He complained that he could not get the particular brand of cigarettes that the salesman represented, in the village where he was prospecting. Whereupon the salesman carefully took his name and address, said he would look into the matter, and gave him a plastic cover for his cigarette packets on the assumption that, in future, he would be able to get them. We then lay down on our berths and settled down for the night.

Having neither bedding roll nor sheet, I simply lay down in my clothes. The train rumbled on towards Bangalore. I thought of the starving people of Bihar, martyrs to the cause of independence, and in the rumbling of the wheels I seemed to hear the pounding of Siva dancing.

7

THE TIGER OF MYSORE

THE BRAND new five-storey hotel in Bangalore is luxury after the grime of the train, and I get a warm welcome from the receptionist so I feel that the inspector was right to recommend it to me. What does it matter if it is, perhaps, a little too new, if the lavatory cistern leaks and there is no hot water in the shower? The bed is soft, and after two nights in trains I am soon asleep.

I awake to the sound of urgent knocking on the door. I turn over, disinclined to answer. But the knocking insists, and so, reluctantly, I drag myself up off the bed to answer it. A smart, athletic-looking man, with a smooth black skin and a brilliant white palm-beach suit, looks down on me as I hitch my sleeping sarong together.

"What is it?" I complain.

"Excuse me, Sir. I am very sorry, Sir."

"But what is it?"

"I don't know how to say it, Sir. Very much regrets there has been such mistakes made by my staff."

"You mean no hot water?"

"No. Not the water. That we cannot help. It is the electricity working the boiler. If there is no electricity, there is no hot water. No mistakes over hot water."

"What is the trouble then? You want my passport?"

"No. Not the passport. You are British, isn't it? The passport is not needed."

"Well, what *do* you want then?"

"I must be giving the apologies on behalf of the management. I hope you will forgive and say no more about it, as you are a gentleman, Sir."

"I wish I knew what you're getting at. I want to go back to sleep."

"Sir, the careless clerk has given you, I fear, a room with an Asian lavatory."

"Oh, good heavens, is that all?"

"If you will come now, Sir, we will change your room immediately."

"Don't get so worried. I don't want to change my room now I've unpacked my things. And I can assure you, I'm quite used to Asian lavatories. I've been in Asian lavatories from Bushire to Bangkok, and I've even been in one in Paris."

"I see. Thank you, Sir."

"But since I'm awake now, I may as well have some breakfast."

"We have four breakfasts, Sir. American, English, Indian and Continental."

"What's the difference between the American and the English?"

"With the American we have fruit juice and with the English fresh fruit."

"I'll have the American."

The manager turned to the room servant to give the order, and then left. It was hot, as the same electricity as had failed the boiler had failed the air-conditioner too. So I went to the windows to open them. But I could not. They were of opaque glass, and fixed into the wall up to a height of six feet, and only the top lights could be opened and shut.

It seemed strange. So I got a chair, climbed onto it, and looked over. Now everything became clear. In the yard below—the yard that one was not supposed to see—there was a truly foul jumble of grass matting huts, blackened cooking pots, bedraggled women and children and scrawny chickens, from which the acrid odour of burning cowdung floated upwards. These, I supposed, were the homes of the untouchables, who were employed to sweep the dust of our rooms with their bunches of grass and reeds—dust which was constantly being swept from place to place, but which I never saw actually being collected in a pan and disposed of at any time.

And the fixed glass, in this hotel of the second half of the twentieth century, was there to prevent the danger of our polluting our eyes with the sight of them, with the vision of these martyrs in the cause of independence when the food shortages get under way.

After breakfast I went straight to the bus station to catch the express for Mysore City eighty-six miles away. Once we were out of Bangalore the bare uplands and great rounded granite outcrops of the Deccan, which looked like huge boulders a thousand feet high, alternated with green and fruitful valleys, with plantations of sugar, mangoes and bananas, as well as the ubiquitous rice. Posters encouraging the growth of various fruit crops slipped by. We passed government institutions for Sericulture, Malaria Training, Fig Culture and many other laudable activities, established in large buildings in bare, empty grounds.

Three-quarters of the way to Mysore we passed through a place called Mandya, where the factory of the Mysore Sugar Company is located. There was a kind of municipal gardens alongside the road, called Jubilee Park 1935 at one end and Mahatma Gandhi Park at the other end, as if to get the best of both worlds. Nearby the "Health Kitchen" advertised "best board apartments", and next to it was the "Hindu Miletry Hotel", catering, I presumed, for soldiers. Road signs said, "Stop, then proceed", and "Sound horn, then proceed", as though afraid that if they simply said "Stop", no one would ever go.

The bus, itself, was strictly non-stop, so that when I tried to get off at Seringapatam, I found it was just not possible. Our one halt to relieve the call of nature had been made purposely out on the open road, and it was clear, as we ran alongside the outer bastions of the island fort, which was my objective, that in spite of my request to the driver, it was going to be our last.

We swept on into Mysore City, which was the capital of the state until the move to Bangalore. It has a long history. When Vijayanagar fell to the Muslims in 1564, Mysore became an independent Hindu state and managed to retain its own identity, ruled by the Wadiyar dynasty. On the high hill overlooking the town they garlanded the huge stone sacred bull with flowers and made sacrifices, sometimes human, to Kali in her local guise as Chamundi in order to ensure their continued prosperity.

Two hundred years later this insurance proved vain when one of the captains of the guard, the famous Muslim, Haidar Ali, seized power. He employed French military advisers, and extended the state's domains. In the western world the hostility between Britain and France showed itself in the latter's support for the Americans in their war of independence. In India the British seized Pondicherry. Haidar Ali, angered at this affront to his ally, marched down to the Carnatic, defeated a British force at Pullalur in 1780 and stood at the very gates of Madras.

These events made the name of Haidar Ali well-known in

England. It is evident from Squire Hardcastle's remarks in Oliver Goldsmith's *She Stoops to Conquer* that his name was on everybody's lips, for the good man says, "There was a time, indeed, I fretted myself about the mistakes of government, like other people; but finding myself every day grow more angry, and the government growing no better, I left it to mend itself. Since that I no more trouble my head about Hyder Ally, or Ally Cawn, than about Ally Croaker."

Haidar Ali died in 1782, and was succeeded by his son, Tipu Sultan, a weaker, less sagacious man than his father. Though the British had not yet joined the struggle against France in Europe, they were virtually at war with her overseas, and so they determined to attack the threat from Mysore at its source. Lord Wellesley, the Governor-General, declared war, Colonel Wellesley, the future Duke of Wellington, marched with the attacking force, and eventually the field was won.

The Wadiyar family was restored by the British to the throne of Mysore, and remained there until 1947. The Wadiyars ruled with the advice of British Residents, and Mysore was commonly regarded, for the best part of a century, as the model of what an "Indian Native State" ought to be. Far from being the antiquated tyrants that the rulers of the states are automatically assumed to have been by certain doctrinaire historians, the rulers of Mysore were so well regarded that, after the accession to the Indian Union, the abdicating Maharaja was made Governor. When the state was doubled in size in 1956 to include Coorg and parts of Hyderabad, Bombay and Madras states, following linguistic divisions, the Maharaja still remained.

The Maharaja's Palace in Mysore City is now a museum, however, for "historical purposes only", as my travelling companion explained, since although it was built as recently as 1897, its function has been taken over by the modern palace in Bangalore. This was where the Maharaja used to show himself to the people at the ten-day autumn festival of Dasahra, which is still celebrated with great pomp and pageantry in Mysore. The Maharaja, now styled Rajpramukh, or "Governor", still sits in a golden howdah on a lavishly painted and caparisoned elephant. He still goes through the main streets of the city, led by a procession of camels, elephants, horses, palanquins, silver coaches and standard bearers. One would imagine that there had been no change in the government.

The first thing that I saw as I walked away from the bus station was the white marble statue of the previous Maharaja, who died in 1940, under its domed canopy supported by four pillars. Behind it there were more domes, rising above the intervening wall and gateway, which floated in the dancing, shimmering air like a fairy-land dream of oriental splendour.

These stood above the main building of the palace, which was once the centre of the web of state. The main gateway, with its ornate pinnacles, is still guarded by the Mysore State Troops in the high red turbans of the Maharaja's uniform, which are reminiscent of an eighteenth-century shako. They levy an entrance fee, though it is possible to go a hundred yards along the wall and enter freely through another gate. The public walk about the wide grounds surrounding the Indo-Saracenic building just like the family groups moving in and out of the great houses of England, but they do not leave so much litter behind them.

I soon found another bus to take me back to Seringapatam, and as we set off my mind went back to the museum in South Kensington where I had first heard of Tipu Sultan. I saw Tipu's wooden tiger on its pedestal in the quiet hall, crouching on a prostrate European in a broad-brimmed, flat-topped black hat with a yellow brim—a servant of the East India Company—and tearing at his throat. Inside the tiger there was a miniature organ, with keyboard and bellows to simulate the roar of the tiger and the groans of the dying man, and a handle to wind it up. Beside this toy Tipu's gold-topped Malacca cane was laid, together with one of the silver medals struck to commemorate the fall of Seringapatam in 1799. Now it was the tiger that was lying underneath, defeated by the British lion with a pennant carrying an inscription in Arabic, *Asad 'ullah al-ghalib*, the Victorious Lion of God, whilst on the reverse the inscription was in Persian, *Srirangapatan-ra 28 zi'l qa'da 1213 hijri khuda dad*. God gave Seringapatam on the 28th of Zi'l Qa'da, in the year of the Hegira 1213.

That was the soul of India to me then—the ferocious sultan and the snarling tiger, the dauntless British troops marching steadfastly past palm and temple to storm the fort perched high above the cliff, from which the fanatic ruler cast his prisoners down, and the natives celebrating their release from despotism with feasts and dancing. This all happened down in the South of India, in the Hindu India of the great temples and the dark-skinned people, a thousand miles from the regions where I did my own military service, and I wanted to see how much of it was true, and how much a story grown out of all proportion in the telling.

The coach in which I travelled was full of Tamil people out on a day tour, complete with canned music and a loudspeaker for the guide. The latter was a college student, studying for his Senior School Leaving Certificate. He wore a woolly white Gandhi cap and spoke in English, saying, "Good morning, my dears" to us although it was half-past-two in the afternoon, but on the subject of Tipu he was non-committal, for Tipu's father had undoubtedly usurped the throne from the Hindu rulers of Mysore, and yet the British were no better. These "English peoples", as he called them, or sometimes simply "the Britishers", had not come to liberate, but simply to conquer the Sultan for their own ends. It was as much as to say, "A plague on both your houses."

Seringapatam is nowadays referred to more accurately as Srirangapatna, for it takes its name from the temple of Vishnu Sri Ranganath, which is much older than the city. Yet it still stands there in the centre of the fort, still alive, still with the wooden chariot for the god, though the fort itself is dead.

In fact the fort was most of the so-called city, which was more of a fortified headquarters for a military regime than a place having the varied functions and life of a real metropolis. It stood at the upstream end of an elongated island formed by the division of the Cauvery river into two streams, and these streams acted as a natural moat and gave it greater strength, for the Cauvery is wide and rocky and swift and the current is strong. The town of Ganjam in the middle of the island could not have been of any great extent.

We went down to the point where the two streams join up again, and from there to the mausoleum of Haidar Ali. It is a large, airy building of white marble, with the minarets and domes that are typically associated with Mogul buildings, set in a formal garden planted with rows of cypress trees. Here Tipu's body was sent to join his father's after he had been shot by a British soldier, whom he had wounded as he tried to get his jewelled sword belt off him. "The light of Islam and the faith left the world," the inscription says. "Tipu became a martyr for the faith of Mohammed. The sword was lost and the son of Haidar fell a noble martyr. A.H. 1213."

Evidently the "Britishers" found it not distasteful too, for the memorial and cemetery to their own dead are also there, though far less magnificent. On the other hand, the beauty of the mausoleum is in extreme contrast with the ugliness of the fort, which Tipu strengthened with the local granite. His idea of making the walls stronger was simply to double the ramparts. He did not heed the counsel of his French advisers, retained the five straight walls and the square bastions that he had inherited from the Hindus, and made his glacis so steep that the attackers could shelter on them from the fire from above.

However, it was only at the second attempt that the fort was taken. The overture was in 1791, when Lord Cornwallis appeared before Seringapatam after the capture of Bangalore. Supply problems forced him to fall back after destroying his battering rams.

Next year he returned with a force of 37,000, of whom 10,000 were Europeans. They were considerable numbers for those days and were equipped with 400 guns. In addition a large band of about 45,000 Mahratta and Hyderabad cavalry had joined him. The fort did not look to me to have had anything like the strength of the high walls of the Old Fort at Delhi or the great bastions of Daulatabad, so that I was not surprised to learn that, when this great force of 82,000 was joined by an additional 9,000 under General Abercrombie, Tipu decided to submit. He surrendered half his territories to the three allies—the British Company, the Hyderabad Nizam and the Mahratta Peshwa—and he handed over his two sons to Lord Cornwallis as hostages.

But the tiger little relished being contained within borders that were not much larger than those of the modern state of Mysore before it was extended in 1956. He conspired with the French, who were now openly at war with the British, and snarled again. Lord Wellesley took up the challenge in 1799. A large body of Tipu's troops was defeated on the western frontier, and after a siege lasting only a fortnight he, himself, was overwhelmed in his own lair in Seringapatam. The town was sacked by the troops, who were both lusting after loot and incensed by the tortures to which the prisoners had been subjected.

Inside the walls of the fort they show you the dungeon in which British prisoners were incarcerated after their capture at Pullalur by Haidar Ali. They also show you the garrison headquarters and "ball alley", the mosque and the plain gravestone, with the star and crescent on it, which marks the spot where Tipu Sultan's body was found. But it is all dead stone. It is only when one leaves the fort and goes down to Tipu's pleasure place beside the river that the picture comes to life.

It is a square, two-storeyed building of modest dimensions, with a low, almost flat roof, and broad verandas all round that reduce its size to that of a small country house. It could hardly be called a palace, as the guide books say. It is a pavilion, surrounded by a graceful garden, and inside the sun screens that fall almost to the level of the floor one can begin to see something of Tipu, the man.

The walls of the pavilion are richly decorated in the Persian manner with arabesque work, and on one side a stylized mural depicts the battle of Pullalur, in which Haidar Ali routed the Company's troops, taking prisoner Colonel Baillie, their commander. The British have formed square. Their rigid ranks in red coats and white trousers, belts and cross braces, looking like the toy lead soldiers of years gone by, are excellently portrayed. The artist has even caught something of the stolid English features in the faces. Inside the square, officers confer on horseback, and another sits in a palanquin, borne by six natives. A gun, attended by two gunners, faces the wrong way, with barrel lowered, and an ammunition wagon blows up. Outside the square a veritable mass of cavalry comes charging in from left and right. Turbaned, moustachioed horsemen, brandishing scimitars, with a few Frenchmen dressed much like the British, attack the square.

During the siege of Seringapatam this mural was defaced. But it was afterwards restored when Colonel Wellesley lived there, and now the whole building is a well-kept museum of those days. Downstairs there is a full model of the fort, made in 1800 from a military survey, with the gateway of the "Great Pagoda" as its highest point. Upstairs a series of prints of "Tipu's droogs" depict the forts perched on the tops of the granite mountain outcrops that were the strong points of his empire.

The prints were published by Captain Allen of 6 Great Marlborough Street as far back as 1794, only three years after the best known fort of them all, Nandidrug, thirty miles to the north of Bangalore, had been captured by the Company's forces. There are also contemporary pencil sketches of Tipu's staff, who do not look like the monsters they have sometimes been called, and in the same room there stands an oil painting of a subject that was to gain a certain vogue in the heroic manner as an episode of empire—Tipu handing over his two sons as hostages to Lord Cornwallis.

All these things remain as they were, and I was interested to see the continuous stream of people passing through the building to look, learn and wonder. They ranged from the large band of school-girls in white blouses and tennis shoes and blue pinafores, conducted by two wrinkled dames in saris and protected by a thick-set tough in khaki carrying a huge, nobbled stick, to the little railway employee from "too much congested" Calcutta, who said he liked travelling because he got free tickets for his holidays.

They had all paid their mite of twenty paisa to get in, and it seemed obvious that with independence many Indians had developed a desire to know about their country and to see its great monuments and historical sites. Previously they would hardly have cared. A few sahibs would have been the only people pottering about these historic rooms. But now the middle classes are switching from the traditional religious pilgrimages to modern style coach tours, taking in famous buildings, natural marvels and beauty spots.

I doubted whether they had any strong feelings about Tipu. The cruelties and outrages of the despot, the enforced circumcisions and conversions to Islam might be forgotten. The gold tiger throne and the royal tigers chained at the entrance to his palace might be remembered. But it was difficult for Hindus to regard him as a real patriot, although he fought the British. Their attitude was more like that of the prime minister, the Dewan Purnaiya, who first served under the Mohammedans, Haidar Ali and Tipu, then under the British, and finally under the restored Hindu Maharaja. For the Mohammedans and the British have come to rule and then gone, but the Hindus continue as before, clinging to their old traditions whenever the rough waves of change seem dangerous, nourishing their great pagodas, turning the blind eye to what they do not wish to see.

In the village that lies between Tipu's fort and his mausoleum there stands a little church that for many years was the home of a man who, in his time, probably learnt and knew more about these same Hindus than any other European.

The Abbé Dubois was ordained in 1792 at the age of twenty-seven, and left France in the same year to work under the guidance of the Missions Etrangères. He thus escaped the French Revolution, when he was sent to Pondicherry to work in southern India. His reputation spread so far that, after the fall of Seringapatam, the future Duke of Wellington asked him to go there to bring back into the faith the Christians who had been forcibly converted to Mohammedanism by Tipu.

This was in spite of the fact that Britain and France were at war, and the Abbé accomplished the task so well that, with this nucleus of 1,800 former apostates, he established the Roman Catholic Church in Mysore. He worked to such good effect that it went from strength to strength. In fact only recently a striking new cathedral was consecrated in Mysore City. Furthermore he was a practical man. He founded agricultural colonies to help the poor, and he promoted vaccination, which was then quite a new thing, so well that over 25,400 people were vaccinated in his time.

Abbé Dubois overcame his converts' prejudices and won their souls by living as one of them and thus gaining their intimacy and confidence. He wore simple white garments and a kind of turban, and lived perfectly simply, although his flock called him Doddhas-wamiayavaru, the "Great Lord". In this way he was able to learn, in his thirty years in India, a tremendous amount about the life of the Hindus, for his converts spoke to him freely about the customs of their ancestors and their way of life.

He was a modest man, who claimed no great merit for his manu-script on "Hindu Manners, Customs and Ceremonies", leaving "to the many learned Europeans residing in the country the task of compiling from authentic documents a more methodical and comprehensive history of the Hindus". But the Governor, Lord William Bentinck, recognized its value and bought it for 2,000 pagodas on behalf of the Company. He said then what might well have been echoed down the years right up to 1947.

"The result of my own observation during my residence in India is that Europeans generally know little or nothing of the customs and manners of the Hindus. We are all acquainted with some prominent marks and facts, which all who run may read; but their manners of thinking, their domestic habits and ceremonies, in which circumstances a knowledge of the people consists, is, I fear, in great part wanting in us."

Abbé Dubois' book fills this want. The English version was first published in 1815, and it has been republished and reprinted ever since. It contains a mass of factual detail on the caste system, the Brahmins and religion, rendered with fairness and understanding, and a lack of bias which is remarkable in a man whose mission in life was to convert the heathen from their idolatry.

Most of the remarks on social conditions that the perceptive Abbé made 150 years ago still have the ring of truth today. He discusses rural indebtedness and shows how, for the three months of the year before the harvest, three-quarters of the inhabitants of the peninsula are on the verge of starvation. He speaks of the rapid increase in population after the stable government of the Europeans had freed southern India from chronic wars. He refers to the Indians' grovelling poverty, and avers that it is hardly possible for any government, however humane, to raise up their circumstances of life to the level prevailing in Europe. He suggests that those who do not believe him should go to study the situation on the spot.

And yet he does not rush into the common error of damning all the customs of the Hindus as either foul or ridiculous. He only calls foul those aspects of the life that thoughtful Hindus would, themselves, condemn, such as the promiscuous "black magic" orgies of some of the Tantric covens, and the barren women who prostitute themselves at the temples in the hopes of fertility, and the hook-swinging and self-mutilation of the fanatics who torture themselves out of devotion to the gods.

Furthermore, to the learned Abbé, well versed in the Classics, these things do not come particularly as a surprise. He is familiar with the pagan practices of the ancient world, as described by authors such as Herodotus and Strabo, and he realises that what he sees in Hindu India is virtually a continuation of that pagan world into modern times. He knows how useless it is to try to impress the Hindus with the miracles of Jesus. They are nothing compared with the wonders performed by Rama in his adventurous life. And as for raising Lazarus from the dead, the Vishnuvites, they say, are doing it all the time.

He believes that the new British regime will be beneficial to the people, but at the same time he puts into a concise epigram what has been true, ever since, in one way or another. "Under the supremacy of the Brahmins," he says, "the people of India hated their government, while they cherished and respected their rulers; under the supremacy of the Europeans they hate and despise their rulers, while they cherish and respect their government."

He mentions the desolation brought about in certain areas by the collapse of the hand-loom industry, which was due to the

9

introduction of machinery into the factories in Europe and the consequent drop in the demand for made-up cotton goods from the East. And finally, he who went to India to convert the natives, and in thirty years worked wonders there, still sees little possibility of change.

"Let us leave them their cherished laws and prejudices," he says, "since no human effort will persuade them to give them up, even in their own interests, and let us not risk making the gentlest and most submissive people in the world furious and indomitable by thwarting them, for, in my opinion, the day when the Government attempts to interfere with any of the more important religious and civil usages of the Hindus will be the past of its existence as a political power."

Successive British Governments heeded well this advice. Some brutal excesses were put down—the burning of widows on their husbands' funeral pyres was outlawed, the traffic in temple women was reduced—but the great amorphous juggernaut of Hinduism was left alone, to fascinate the contemplative with its spirituality and the lubricious with its sensuality, ready for a new outburst of enthusiasm at the time of independence and after.

The gentle Abbé laboured long and hard, as so many others have done since, in that peculiar love-hate relationship with the Indians that has shown itself so often in those who have gone East of Suez out into the midday sun. And on his return to Paris, as others on their return to London or Cheltenham, he might have echoed the words of a nineteenth-century Italian bishop: "*La caldaia è molto grande, ma la carne è molto poca*"—The cooking pot is very big, but there's very little meat.

Naturally the Abbé meant nothing to the little dark Tamil people in the bus, and we departed without delay in the direction of Mysore City. But on the far side of the Cauvery river we turned right and followed a straight road for about ten miles to a point further upstream. A problem that had been worrying me was then solved, for seeing how swift and turbulent the river was, even in March, the dry season of the year, I could not understand how the Company's troops had been able to cross it under fire to storm Tipu's fortress.

The fact is that a great dam, one and three-quarter miles long, the Krishnaraja Sagar, now lies across the river, and releases water through the hydro-electric power station at Sivasamudram in a continuous flow. In Tipu's day the river would have been almost dried out in April and May, the time of year both sieges of Seringapatam took place, although a smaller dam, built by Haidar Ali, was already in existence.

The modern dam, with the Brindavan gardens below it, is a popular place for weekend family outings, and deservedly so, for the long, sloping vista of the gardens, sparkling with rows of fountains, leading down to the lake at the bottom, which is sprayed with powerful jets of water rising in long arcs high into the air, is more impressive, even, than the famous Shalimar gardens in Kashmir, on which it is modelled. And when the illuminations go on at night, a gasp goes up from the crowd as the whole place seems to be transformed into a fairyland.

The dam and its beautiful adornments were all the work of the Maharaja's Government, and named after his able prime minister. And thereby hangs a mystery, for if India in those days could build great public works without foreign aid, why is it that today no such undertaking gets under way without big loans of foreign money and expertise? The vast ruins that lie scattered all over India from end to end are the evidence that the country never lacked the ability to build on the grand scale from her own resources.

We stopped for refreshment at the "Travellers' Hotel" just before reaching the dam. It was self-service, and I tried a spicy fried cake with a glass of excellent coffee, whilst most of the others got their right hands stuck into a mush of fried rice on a leaf. Then we drove along the top of the dam on a road that was wide enough for two buses to pass, and down the slope to the bottom end of the gardens, where forty or fifty buses were parked in rows.

The Tamils, who are continually increasing in numbers in Mysore over the longer established Kanarese, were most in evidence. Little girls ran up with their begging tins, happily pestering one until one dropped them a coin, but hardly serious about it. They simply seemed to be having a game. Instead of playing ball, they were playing begging, and the white man on his own was the obvious target. The boys begged less attractively but more insistently, offering little guide books and packets of postcards, and attaching themselves to one for half the length of the gardens, looking up with frightened, soulful eyes that seemed to say that they would get no dinner if they went home to their fathers without making a sale.

As usual the beggars took the edge off the enjoyment of a noble scene, and I was not sorry when I was able to find a spare seat in a Wells Fargo luxury coach returning to Bangalore. Its "luxuries" included red and green port and starboard lights in front as well as the conventional side and head lamps, and at the back there was a colourful, illuminated shrine of some local deity. Behind the driver's seat there was a water urn with a plastic tumbler, together with a record player, whilst above his head there were photographs of three men who have gone into history—the two Prime Ministers, Nehru and Shastri, with President Kennedy between them.

We set off into the night with the record player roaring. Then it was silenced to allow us to doze. But I was still awake as we swept past the silent grey walls of Seringapatam, and I tried to visualize what it had been like when the strong man, Haidar Ali, was there. I thought of his son, Tipu, who had not the strength of character or sagacity to maintain what his father had built up—of Tipu and his tigers, of the English sailors and soldiers who had been forcibly circumcised and made to join his forces, of the final irony of "Citizen Tipu" despatching his embassy to the champions of liberty and equality in the French Republic, and of the letter Napoleon sent to him from Cairo in the full flood of his ambitions in the orient "to the most Magnificent Sultan, our greatest friend Tipu Sahib. You have already been informed of my arrival on the borders of the Red Sea, with an innumerable and invincible army, full of the desire of delivering you from the iron yoke of England. . . . May the Almighty increase your power and destroy your enemies."

In the event Tipu's powerful ally could not save him, and the French power in India never recovered. The British were determined that the French should never again be in a position to hand over their English prisoners to the mercy of Indian tyrants, and they remained confined to their five small settlements on the coasts.

QUEEN VICTORIA VERY GOOD MAN

THE WATER in the rose on the shower has given out with a throaty gurgle, and I call up the reception desk by telephone. Presently five men come to look at it—the manager, the assistant manager, the room servant, the waiter and the lift boy. We discuss the subject for ten minutes.

"Perhaps a plumber might deal with the matter?" I suggest. "Perhaps the fault is not even in the room at all? Perhaps it is the main water supply that has failed? Perhaps they might see whether the water is flowing in the other rooms or not?"

All these are interesting suggestions, received with happy smiles. "What a gentleman this man is!" the smiles seem to say. "To think of so many possibilities." They stand round me in an admiring semi-circle as I sit with my modesty scarcely covered by the bath towel I had been hoping to take off to have my shower.

"Well," I say. "What about it?"

"Yes. It is a possibility. Do not worry."

"I mean, could we . . .?"

"We are seeking the solution. Everything will be in order."

"Could you bring up some buckets or something?"

"We have to consider first why it is not working."

"Yes. Let's do that."

"It may be the electricity again."

"I thought that only affected the hot water."

"There is, perhaps, a pump."

"Yes. Perhaps there is a pump."

By this time I wanted to give up the idea of having a shower and get dressed. But there they were, standing round me, gazing with steady, beady eyes.

"I don't think I'll have a shower after all," I said.

The assistant manager's eyes filled with compassion. "But, Sir, you must be taking shower. It is your right. Do not worry. I will arrange."

"Good."

The five pairs of eyes remained just where they were.

"I think I'll be getting dressed now," I said.

"Please!" The eyes did not move.

"You must be busy."

"Oh no, Sir. We are at your service. All times at your service."

"Then?"

"If you will allow me. One moment."

The assistant manager walked into the bathroom, and turned on the tap of the shower. There was another gurgle, then a double thump in the pipe, and then a rush of water out of the shower, which drenched the right arm of his palm-beach suit. The eyes that, all along, had been convinced of their own superiority, looked at me again.

"There, Sir. You should have asked the bearer how to work it. You are seeing the tap? You must turn the tap on."

"Turn tap on!" I repeated it like a child of four. "I see!"

"Do not hesitate to enquire. You are wanting anything, we are all at your service, gentleman!"

The five men padded, silent-footed, out of the room again. I had my shower, then walked out of the hotel, past the Gurkha doorman, who stood all day and half the night by the main door, held in a strait-jacket of inactivity. Skirting round the dusty wall of the race-track, I encountered nobody but the poor and lowly, and it was the same on the wide road in an avenue of trees that led towards the parade-ground and the park, although it was mid-morning. I went past a group of cows nuzzling at some old leaves, that looked like discarded food plates, and past old men and women squatting on the roadside trying to sell little over-ripe bananas and handfuls of dusty old peanuts. An ambulance clanked slowly past, ringing its bell loudly, although there was no casualty inside, and that was all the traffic I saw, until I turned left into Post Office Road, where some of the Japanese style three-wheeler taxis were chugging along behind their khaki-clad drivers.

A mass of notices of government offices met my eyes, written in English, with the version in Kanarese, the local language, underneath. Amongst them were the State Information Centre, the Directorate of Animal Husbandry, the Office of the Director of

Sericulture, the Office of the Director of Industries and Commerce, and most necessary in this proliferation of bureaucracy, the
Government Stationery Department. Yet another official notice
met my gaze, which must be no less necessary, if the continual
accusations of corruption in government business are to be believed.
It was the Office of the State Vigilance Commissioner.

This conglomeration of large signs disfigured the side of the road
as commercial advertisements might in another country. One
wondered what all these various departments of government
actually did, and why a lorry loaded with bales of hay was going
into the office compound of the Executive Engineer of the Mysore
State Electricity Board. One wondered why the Vidhana Soudha,
the enormous State Assembly building, surmounted by the golden
lions of Asoka, had not room to house these executive branches of
government as well. Perhaps it was too handsome, too elegant
behind the double avenue of cypress trees and lamp standards, to
concern itself with the merely practical business of administration.

In the park men were squatting in large groups in the shade of
the big banyan trees and the purple jacarandas, getting their full
measure of Sunday rest. The Mysore government museum on the
other side of it was well frequented too, and there was a steady
stream of people wandering in past the two huge grimacing doorkeepers with garlands of human heads and trident staffs with
grinning skulls on them.

Here, as at Seringapatam, there were old prints done only a few
years after Bangalore had been taken by the East India Company.
These were of the old fort of Bangalore and its surroundings,
published in 1804 by Edwarde Orme, His Majesty's printseller of
59 New Bond Street, London. There were also twelfth-century
Hoysala sculptures from Halebid, half-way to the west coast, and
there was a four-headed statue of Brahma, the creator, with a
crown covering all four heads together and a goatee beard and
stiff horizontal moustache on each face, looking like a Portuguese
fidalgo.

But the most interesting section of this museum, which was
completed as recently as 1962 at a cost of Rupees 325,000, was the
part upstairs devoted to the life of Mahatma Gandhi. His earlier
letters on non-violence and on the theory of passive resistance, to
C. F. Andrews, Annie Besant and Tolstoy were displayed there,
as well as more recent documents of great historic interest to India,

such as his letter of July 1st, 1942 to Roosevelt, offering co-operation against the Japanese if he could coerce the British into granting immediate independence, which was delivered to the American President by Louis Fischer. The photographs of Gandhi showed him with Sir Stafford Cripps, with Lord Pethick-Lawrence, with Earl and Lady Mountbatten, and with others of the great political figures of his time, who were concerned with Indian affairs.

As I walked round these exhibits, I thought I heard again the endless argument that used to rage about this slight, gnome-like figure, bare-headed, bare-chested, clad only in the white dhoti hanging in a loop over each leg. Was he saint or charlatan, saviour or rabble-raiser, great idealist or casuistic lawyer?

Perhaps the true answer is that he was all these things at once. The humility of his self-elected poverty, of his rule of always travelling third-class on the railways, of wearing peasant clothes, of eating nothing but the simplest food, was matched by his arrogance in assuming the role of mentor and conscience of millions of people. His devotion to non-violence was, itself, expressed in fighting terms, such as the struggle for independence and the "Quit India" campaign of 1942, and when the goal of independence was achieved, it was in such a blood bath of violence that the dead were more numerous than all the casualties of the Second World War. Though he remained true to his own ideals, he could use arguments of Jesuitical casuistry to further them. Perhaps the most practical of his exhortations to the Indian people was that, even if they could not be persuaded to dig latrines, they might at least equip themselves with trowels to bury their own excreta. It went unheeded.

It I were a modern Plutarch, it would be in such antithetical terms as these that I would have to write his life, for this most Indian of Indians derived most of his philosophy from abroad. His devotion to the peasant ideal was inspired by Tolstoy. He wrote to him at Yasnaya Polnaya as disciple to master, and his dreams of the ideal community of peasant villages were initially derived from the later teachings of the renegade Russian aristocrat. Though regarded as a Hindu saint, he himself has said that his spiritual delight came to him from studying and reflecting on Christ's Sermon on the Mount, whilst his first knowledge of the Bhagavad Gita, which is sometimes compared to that sermon by philosophers, was obtained through Sir Edwin Arnold's English translation.

Yet through all these paradoxes shone the man himself, utterly devoted to the good, loving his adversaries as much as his allies and much more than himself. He was, perhaps, the most perfect example of what he, himself, has described as a *yogi* of action, as compared with the yogi of meditation.

"The *karma yogi*," he said, "is a devotee who is jealous of none, who is a fount of mercy, who is without egotism, who is selfless, who treats alike cold and heat, happiness and misery, who is ever forgiving, who is always contented, whose resolutions are firm, who has dedicated mind and soul to God, who causes no dread, who is not afraid of others, who is free from exultation, sorrow and fear, who is pure, who is versed in action yet remains unaffected by it, who renounces all fruit, good or bad, who treats friend and foe alike."

And concerning that action Gandhi's view was that it was better to travel than to arrive, that the importance lay in the journey and not in the goal. "He who is ever brooding over result," he wrote, "often loses nerve in the performance of duty. He becomes impatient and then gives vent to anger and begins to do unworthy things; he jumps from action to action, never remaining faithful to any. He who broods over results is like a man given to the objects of senses; he is ever distracted, he says good-bye to all scruples, everything is right in his estimation and he therefore resorts to means fair or foul to attain his end."

Mahatma Gandhi's assassin was an example of this kind, but the people of India gave their verdict when they attended his funeral in a vast array.

I left the museum and walked a hundred yards, past the new Visvesvaraya Industrial and Technological Museum, to the beginning of the Mall, which runs along the south side of the parade-ground. But it is not called the Mall any longer, although the statue of Queen Victoria still stands there facing down it. It is called Mahatma Gandhi Road like so many other main streets in India, giving Gandhi equal remembrance in the cantonment with Sir Mark Cubbon, the first commissioner, whose road runs along the other side of the parade-ground.

The shops were shut, and the whole of the broad road and pavement had an air of deserted Sunday calm about it as if it really were still part of a British cantonment on the sabbath day. A short way along the shopping side of the road I came across the premises of the Bible Society, with the posters of the Scripture Gift Mission nearby, exhorting one to believe in the Lord Jesus Christ and be saved, whilst across the empty, brown expanse of the parade-ground I could see the off-white square tower of Saint Andrew's Kirk of the Scottish Church of South India, which is over 100 years old.

Originally the cantonment was two miles from the city, far enough away for the new rulers to keep themselves aloof from the crowds and stenches and pestilences, but near enough to have easy access for control and commerce. It soon grew to be the equal in area of the city, though far smaller in population, with its large open spaces, broad roads and bungalows set in spacious gardens. Now the division between the Petta, as the city is called, and the cantonment has largely been obscured as the gap between them has been progressively filled in by government buildings, clubs and residential areas. Yet the cantonment atmosphere, though subtly changed by the change from British to Indian dominance, still remains.

I found myself comparing this cantonment with the other cantonments I had known—the large ones like Delhi and Lahore, and the small ones like Rawalpindi and Jhelum. They had all been laid out on simple, practical principles of town planning, with wide, straight roads lined with avenues of trees, intersected by smaller residential avenues. The main thoroughfare, with its shops and churches, hospital and club, was usually called the Mall. The smaller roads were named after governors or generals or com-missioners or official buildings such as the Post Office or the Residency, and the bungalows sat serenely in their English gardens made with Indian trees and flowers.

All this happened long before town and country planning was taken seriously in the homeland, and the break with the former way of life in India was complete, for the British felt so secure, and indeed had become so secure, in their occupation of the country, that they no longer felt the need to live in forts and behind fortified defences, as their ancestors and previous conquerors had done. The age of English family life in India began in earnest. Wives and daughters travelled P. and O. in large numbers through the Suez canal to join the men, who were bearing the white man's burden, and set up house in the wilds of India with no more protection than a night watchman and a dog asleep on the veranda.

But at the same time as the defence fortifications went down, the social barriers went up. Colourful characters like Job Charnock, who snatched his eventual wife from the flames just as she was about to be thrown on the funeral pyre of her dead husband, belonged to the past. The memsahibs expected their menfolk to marry people like them, and not to mix with the Indians except for formal social occasions out in the open. As for the woman of mixed blood, she was even worse according to the social code that then existed. The beautiful Eurasian became the *femme fatale*, heaven to a man in a clandestine affair, but hell to marry and ruin to his career.

It was little wonder, then, that a sense of resentment grew large in the normally tolerant minds of Indians. To mix freely in the social life of London and Hurlingham, and then to be snubbed in a railway carriage in one's own country by some ignorant tax-collector's wife was more than any man could reasonably be expected to stand. So it was better to keep apart, to be wary, not to reveal one's true feelings—an attitude difficult for people who are characteristically the most loquacious, transparent and warm-hearted in the world.

When I went into my first cantonment in the Punjab, the situation was changing once again. Indians were in administrative positions in the government and, more important to me, they were also being commissioned into the army as officers in increasing numbers. Thinking Englishmen agreed that it was not fair, and thinking Scotsmen said that it was not right that they should remain excluded from the clubs. Only a minority of diehards amongst the old *koi hais* remained to plead that the British had built the clubs for themselves, and they did not see why the Indians couldn't set up their own clubs if they wanted to.

The difficulty was that the typical cantonment was a small community, largely made up of the various ranks and grades of officialdom, and subject to the social stresses and strains of any small group. These were complicated by the differences of race and religion, and of family customs and social habits, such as we are beginning to see revealed in our own country by the immigrants of today.

The Indian tended to keep his own wife in the background, yet felt slighted if the memsahib turned away when he got too close. On the one hand he wanted to join the club because it was the nerve centre of the rulers, yet on the other hand he felt that, by doing so, he was turning himself into a lackey in another way. He wanted to drink to show that he could take it like the hardened habitués, yet he probably actually preferred an orange juice or a cup of sweet tea.

These are wild generalizations, of course, which can be disproved a hundred times. Yet I know that they are true, because many of the newly commissioned Indian officers told me so, with that lack of reticence, which is one of the most endearing qualities that the Indians bring to life.

I remember one occasion on which one of our Indian officers had been drinking with us in the club. There came a time when we saw clearly that he could not take it any more, but what we did not see so clearly was that we, ourselves, could hardly take it any better.

We went back to our quarters—a row of cell-like rooms in a wartime bamboo building—and gathered on the veranda round a bottle of whisky which someone had produced from his kit. The Indian drank with us. The talk grew loud and animated, and soon it turned into a discussion about this strange land, to which we had been transported straight from school. We had been told about the rivalry between the Hindus and the Muslims, which was apt to get worse in the hot weather, when any small incident might spark off a riot, so it was natural to get on to the subject of these two religions.

"The difference between the Muslims and the Hindus," said one young man, who thought he knew all the answers, "is that the Muslims just have one God, but the Hindus have hundreds of different ones. So the Muslims are really more like us. And the Hindus worship all sorts of peculiar gods with a whole lot of arms and heads, and they worship animals too, and anything you like to think of, and even sex. They worship that too. It's fantastic!"

The Indian had kept silent up till now, and it seemed that the speaker had forgotten he was there. But the next moment he repeated his words directly to the Indian's face. "It's fantastic," he said. "Even put up an old stone somewhere, and they'll worship it."

At that the Indian got to his feet. "Very fantastic!" he said. "Very, very fantastic. And now I am telling you the most fantastic thing of all." His voice rose into a high-pitched gabble. "The people who worship this!" He flung his arms out wide, with his

fingers outstretched at their ends, and hung his head on one
side in a terrible grimace of misery. "This," he said. "This is
fantastic."

"What are you getting at?" the other subaltern said. "What's
that supposed to be?"

"Don't you know? Can't you recognize it?" He put on the
grimace again like a caricature of agony. "That's your Jesus Christ,
and you don't recognize it? You complain of our strange gods, and
I am asking you, what could be stranger than worshipping a
miserable figure nailed to a piece of wood and dying on it? We
have many gods because we worship life, and life has many forms.
And I am asking you, what do you worship? Death!"

There was a sudden silence on the veranda. The Englishman
stared at the Indian, horrified that he should dare to criticize the
religion of the masters like a blasphemer. The Indian remained
there with his arms outstretched, grimacing in a mock misery that,
as every second passed, appeared to become more and more a real
emotion. Slowly the hands dropped and the arms went back to the
sides. He turned away.

"You're not going, are you?" I said. "No reason why you
shouldn't have your say."

"I am going to bed now to dream of all these fantastic things,"
he answered.

"Oh, I say," the one who had started it all said. "No hard
feelings. Let's forget it."

But the Indian walked away to his cell of a room and left us to
ourselves.

The incident came vividly to my mind as I walked round the
parade-ground to the Scots Kirk. There were not many people in
the congregation to sing the slow, lugubrious hymns, for all it
consisted of was about a dozen British faces and the same number
of Indians. When one sang, one heard one's own voice clearly
against the thin background.

The minister spoke about the elections, and about how necessary
it was to become involved in the affairs of the nation, to give the
people knowledge of themselves so that they might have the chance
of living in human dignity. He talked about a group of European
church social workers, who had worked for five years in a certain
village, and at the end of five years they at last persuaded the
villagers to subscribe a sum of money, which the government

doubled, to set up a peanut factory. And then they turned Communist. "All the same," he said. "They had found dignity."

An old-timer was sitting in front of me, nodding in the heat. He sat through the last hymn, then got up to go. I followed him out. The sun was blazing down on the road, and the three-wheeler taxis all seemed to have melted into the ground, so I had to walk again. This time it was to the West End Hotel, and the refuge of the shaded veranda and the cool dining-room. Food restriction was in force, meaning that, if one had an A Course, which was the main dish, one could only have one B Course. After some study of the menu I concluded that the net result of Food Restriction was that I would be able to have either curds or mango fool, but not both. It did not seem to be very severe hardship.

Here in the West End Hotel and in the Bangalore Club the cantonment life continues. It is still the European and Christian holidays that are the festive occasions—Christmas and New Year more important than Deepavali and Dasahra. The fancy-dress balls and the baby shows preserve the old customs, and the cocktail parties carry on with the gin and whisky merely more diluted.

These affairs are all faithfully reported in the *Onlooker*, which still flourishes like its glossy counterpart in London, the *Tatler*. Calcutta Causerie and Madras Musings, the Voice of Delhi, Gateway Gossip from Bombay, and the notes from Bangalore tells us who is entertaining whom in the social world of diplomats, business leaders and military men; who is getting married (but not who is getting divorced), who is having a birthday party, promoting an airline or opening a new hotel.

Flipping through the glossy pages, I see that in Bombay "another gay party with sumptuous dinner and beverages was given by attractive Shirin Soonawala to celebrate the birthday of her husband Edul whose excellent floral arrangement could not fail to catch the discerning eye. Enjoying the Soonawalas' hospitality were Mr and Mrs B. S. Nadkarni, Assistant Income-Tax Commissioner, Mr and Mrs Hooseini Doctor, Dr and Mrs N Vazifdar, Capt. Avinash Kohli, Mr R. Ghista of Sarabhai Chemicals and the Consul General of Yugoslavia and Mrs Bulat."

I read that in Calcutta the Maharaja, whom I used to meet chatting up my landlady in Darjeeling, has given the reception of the season for the wedding of his daughter, with a guest list "that could have been a major portion of Calcutta's *Who's Who*

from the diplomatic corps to business magnates and racing person-
alities."

In Madras, I see, an International Evening of Music, Song and
Dance, organized by the Guild of Service (Central) as their main
annual money-raising effort, "was a thumping success thanks to
the inspiring leadership of Mrs Mary Clubwala." Meanwhile
from Delhi an Australian party is reported with an invitation that
read, "Holy Cow! It's on again. For Saddhus, Saints, Satyrs,
Gnomes and Nymphets. Guests to be dressed likewise."

The news from Bangalore is rather more sedate, and the longest
paragraph describes the hotel, in which I, myself, am staying. It is
reported to contain "telephones with extensions into highly functional modern bathrooms", an air-conditioned bar, "stocking the
choicest of Indian and imported liquors and an array of Indian,
Continental, Chinese and Moghlai cuisine", and a roof-garden
available for private parties. The cost? Rupees 2,500,000, of which
Rupees 500,000 were advanced by the government out of public
funds.

However, the gay time is not forgotten in the account of the
fancy-dress masked ball on New Year's Eve at the United Services
Club. "Costumes were original and amusing. The trio representing
Vat 69, Spencer's Soda and a tumbler, won first prize, and Mrs
Sita Bhatija, one of Bangalore's leading lady doctors, together with
her team Dr Loopless (holding a baby doll!), Dr Slaughter and
Dr Gas Bag, were a popular second."

So the revels carry on from year to year, reported in all their
most inane particulars by the monthly glossy magazine that claims
to be "India's finest". Thus Madras can see what Bombay is doing,
and Delhi can see what Calcutta and Bangalore are up to, and they
can all read about each other, and more important, about themselves
in this eddy of a former whirl which swirls the little social group
around.

In the early evening I went to visit a Parsi family, who have been
prominent in the club life of Bangalore ever since the Second
World War. I got into a three-wheeler and gave the address, but
the driver did not seem to understand, although I repeated the
name of the road several times in standard English. Grant Road
seemed to mean nothing to him, and it meant no more to the next
driver I hailed, so once again I found myself walking. I studied the
street plan of the cantonment in my tourist pamphlet, and saw that

it could not be far, but it was dark and I became uncertain of my way. I turned to two well-dressed young men, who were walking my way, and asked them for directions.

"Can you tell me how to get to Grant Road?" I said.

They both looked up at me. "We are going that way," one of them said. "You come with us, please. Whom do you want to see?"

"I am visiting friends."

"Which house is it, please?"

"Just show me Grant Road and I shall be quite all right."

"You are probably wanting Number 98, isn't it?"

"Not at all. Why should I want Number 98?"

"Are you sure you are not wanting Number 98?"

"Quite sure."

"Then why are you going to Grant Road, please?"

"I am just going to visit some friends," I said. "Is this the way?"

"We have been telling you this is the way. Why are you not believing us?"

"I do believe you. I was just making sure."

"Don't worry. Don't worry. Each and every place you want to go, we will take you."

"Very kind of you. Perhaps you would tell me who you are."

"I am working in the aircraft industry, and my friend here—he is a lawyer. Just you come with us."

"Are you going to Grant Road, then?"

"Not to say exactly Grant Road. We may be. Nearby perhaps. Number 98 is not easy to find."

"Why not?"

"It is not next to Number 97 or Number 96. It is difficult if you have not been there before."

"I have not been there before, and I'm not going there either," I replied rather sharply.

"Why don't you go to the Garden Hotel? That is a good place."

"I am not going to Number 98 or the Garden Hotel!" I began to raise my voice. I looked again at my paper plan. "All I want is Grant Road!"

A pained look passed across the face of the man in the aircraft industry. "What are you wanting to look at that for?" he pleaded. "Are you not trusting us, Sir?"

"Are we nearly there?"

"Look! We are here. Why are you worrying so much? Look!"

Madurai—Dancing Siva

Madurai—(*above*)
young mouths to feed.
(*left*) Pagoda of the
Fish-eyed Goddess

He gazed at me as if he were speaking to a child. "That sign. I am reading it for you. It says Grant Road."

"Ay, it does! Thank you very much. Goodbye!" Without actually breaking into a run, I fled with giant strides.

The bungalow I sought was near the brewery, past a hairdresser's parlour. But not knowing from which end I had entered the road, I was still at a loss and walked the length of the wall of the brewery before concluding that I had gone too far. As I passed the hairdresser's bungalow for the second time, a woman's voice, thick and sarcastic, called out from the darkened compound, "Up the British!"

I could just see the dark outline of a woman's shape on the other side of the low wall, but I did not stop to answer. It seemed better to assume that the shout was not meant for me, and to go on up the side road to find the bungalow that I was looking for.

The three sisters were there, and welcomed me as best they could for the sake of a mutual friend from wartime days. But it was not easy for them as Zarina had an arm in plaster, and Nurghesh had hardly recovered from a bout of influenza. Diana, the only one of the three who was married, had moved in to nurse them.

I keenly appreciated their hospitality, the more so as two of them were writers after their fashion, regular contributors to the Bangalore weekly magazine, *Mysindia*. Zarina was responsible for writing up the news of club balls and fancy-dress parties, whilst Nurghesh was a poetess in the gently satirical vein. Here is Nurghesh Kothawala on the famine situation in Bihar:

> Madhu Limaye criticized the "craze
> Of the Ministers and leaders of the Congress
> To make aerial surveys
> To assess
> The Bihar drought situation." He went on to say
> That even from 200 yards away
> One could not expect
> To get a picture correct,
> So in an aerial survey
> It would be impossible to assess
> The damage to crops. He spoke
> Bitterly to the Press,
> Saying it seemed a "cruel joke."
> . . . But Mr Limaye, even if from a 'plane
> One tries in vain
> To get a clear

10

Idea,
Please don't feel apprehensive!
Though these air flips extensive
May be futile and expensive,
You must not say that no purpose they serve;
For our Ministers, weighed down with care,
Surely deserve
Some relaxation and fresh air.
Mr Limaye, enough of your taunts—
Let them have these *uplifting* jaunts!

These poems, tilting mildly at inept bureaucracy, worldly politicians and chaotic administration, were a good sign. At least they showed that the right to criticize and the freedom of the press were still very much upheld in India, and that it was not yet a crime to laugh at and prod the rulers.

At the Kothawalas we discussed old times, and the drinks and cocktail snacks were handed round. The Brigadier and his wife, who were with us, looked back nostalgically at the times they had spent in England. None of them knew if they would ever see the West again, for under the foreign exchange regulations, it was almost impossible to travel far without breaking the law. And they were sad, living in their own land, yet not unlike exiles. They looked back, and there did not seem to be any future.

This time I was lucky enough to find a taxi to take me on my way. We drove out of Grant Road up Residency Road and Brigade Road, and along Mahatma Gandhi Road beside the parade-ground. At the far end we skirted round the old statue.

"Who is that?" I said to the driver.

"That is Queen Victoria," he answered. "Queen Victoria very good man!"

9

THE COMMUNIST STATE

THE PLANE heads south-west towards the Malabar coast, and
the land looks as dry and drab as any of the wide, sunbaked land-
scapes of the Indian countryside. We cross the winding reaches
of the Cauvery river and hillsides that are either completely bare
or clothed in a sparse scrub that hardly covers their nakedness.
The only roads are rough dirt tracks, and the earth-coloured
buildings of the villages are huddled together as if for mutual
protection.

But then a sudden change takes place. The land falls away into
a wide, fertile plain. White houses and churches are dotted about
the green fields. We land at Coimbatore, and take off again over
more uplands. Once again the hills fall away, this time to an even
richer, greener plain, criss-crossed by a maze of waterways. It is
a land of paddy fields and clumps of tall coconut-palms, more
like Thailand or Malaya than any part of India that I have seen
before. It is the Communist state of the Indian Union called
Kerala. But the Communism there is nothing like the Communism
we fought for eight years in Malaya.

When I arrived in Kerala, the state that was formed out of
Travancore, Cochin and the other native states of the south-
western tip of India, together with the Malabar region of the Madras
Presidency and the ports of Cochin and Quilon, which were
enclaves belonging to British India, the Communists had just
come to power in alliance with the normally conservative Muslims.
Like the Hindus of the South, who are divided into the sects of
the Left Hand and the Right Hand, the Communists of India
are also divided. The left wing Communists follow the Pekin line,
calling themselves the real Marxists, whilst the right wing Communists look to Moscow for inspiration.

This was the second time the Communists had come to power in

47

Kerala. The first Communist Government there lasted for a year from 1965 until the Government of India in Delhi took over, taking the administration into its own hands because of civil strife and reported maladministration. But the electorate again declared their disillusionment with the Congress Party when they voted them out of office in the elections of 1967.

The new Communist Government was a coalition of the left and right wings, with the left wing, led by Mr Namboodiripad, the Chief Minister, in the ascendant. This may seem surprising when one considers the prestige the Soviet Union enjoys in India against the disillusionment with China after the frontier war of 1962, but basically it was logical, for it echoed Kerala's revolt against Delhi and the bourgeois Congress Party and all it stands for. Kerala is the most fertile, productive and literate of all the Indian states, and its Malayali people did not see why they should provide a large slice of India's export revenue with their plantation crops, and yet be denied the imports that could convert the state from the bullock-cart and rowing-boat to the automobile and outboard-engine age.

In addition to his attacks on the Congress handling of the food situation and his complaints about not receiving a fair share of the development projects subsidized by the Central Government, the new Chief Minister has asserted that the separate Indian states should have the right to have direct dealings with foreign governments, which would include the right to export where they liked, and to use the foreign exchange for their own imports instead of having to make do with the Government of India allocations. It would also include the right to form a direct link with China.

One may wonder why this green and pleasant land, out of all the states of India, has chosen to go Communist twice running, whereas the heart-breaking despair of the dust bowls of the North has hardly brought a trickle down that stream.

The answer is threefold. Firstly, although the land is fertile, so are the people, and the population density is such that, even with the high yield, there is hardly enough food to go round. Secondly, the state is small, and the spread of political ideas throughout the land in city streets and country coffee-shops is easier than it could ever be in the vast spaces of the bigger states, whilst the large groups of landless plantation labourers, considered to be almost untouchables by the caste-conscious Nayars, are fruitful fields for the political agitators to till. Thirdly, the people are intelligent and, for India, highly literate, and know that poverty and famine need not necessarily be parts of the inevitable cycle of reproduction and destruction. Perhaps the most hopeful sign for the future is the contraceptive factory that is being built in the state capital, Trivandrum.

I saw nothing of all this when my plane landed at Cochin. My travelling companion was a priest in a white robe and a black pillbox hat, belonging to the large community of Christians who form nearly a quarter of the state's population. They trace their origins back to the Syrians, who left Asia Minor as refugees in the fifth century after the Council of Ephesus had declared their Nestorian form of worship to be heretical, and although many switched to Rome under Portuguese pressure at the time of the Inquisition, contact is still maintained with the Bishop of Antioch.

The young priest told me he was still studying his theology, and hoped to go soon to Boston University to present his thesis. I supposed he might find a fellow-feeling between his own sect's resistance to the power of Rome and that most protestant of American cities.

We parted at the airport, where a group of British planters, waiting for their friends, stood out amongst the slight, dark Malayalis. They seemed very self-possessed, undismayed by the latest twist of the political wheel, and stoically confident in their ability to control their own folk, like prefects at a public school when the fourth form gets unruly.

I left them in order to drive down the island on which the airport stands. It is all flat, with the road running alongside the railway as far as the terminus and then continuing on its own to the end of the land. The distance is about two miles, yet the whole of the island was reclaimed from the sea in this century and named after Lord Willingdon, the Viceroy at the time. The town of Cochin, itself, which is the earliest European settlement in India, is on another island facing the Arabian sea, whilst the much larger town of Ernakulam, which used to be the capital of Cochin State, is spread out along the shore of the mainland opposite.

From the northern tip of Willingdon Island it was possible to see both ways. To the east lay the waterfront of Ernakulam, with here and there the white block of a new concrete hotel breaking the skyline across the lagoon, whilst to the west, across a much narrower stretch of water, stood the crowded shoreline of old Cochin.

But this was not all. There were more islands to the north, enclosing the lagoon and restricting access to the sea to an entrance only 150 yards wide, which had to be specially deepened to allow modern ships to enter. In fact there is a network of islands stretching nearly the whole length of the Kerala coast, like the lace frills on the hem of a petticoat, which makes it possible for small boats to thread their way through the backwaters to Quilon for a distance of eighty miles as the crow flies. If they went out to sea, they would risk being swamped, especially when the monsoon blows across from Africa.

I went into the Malabar Hotel at the end of the artificial island, and a raucous cawing of crows hit my ears, dry and insistent like a consumptive cough. They were large black creatures with feathers that had long ago lost their gloss and sheen, hopping from tree to windowsill and windowsill to the ground, where they strutted for a few seconds before taking off again. A long wooden veranda on the first storey led to the rooms, and at the end of it sat a little man with a sewing machine, ready to mend collars and stitch cuffs for a few paisa.

The rooms themselves belonged to the spacious days before air-conditioning. There were curtains of wooden balls threaded on strings hanging over the windows. But the crows had grown used to them. As I opened the door of my room, one of them removed its beak from the jug of milk left over from the previous occupant's breakfast, looked at me with its head on one side, then ambled slowly across the table and hopped through the red, white and green balls out on to the windowsill.

I wasted no time going out again, for the public jetty was only a stone's throw from the hotel gate, and there were boats waiting to take people across to the island of Cochin. It was, perhaps, fortunate that it was only a few hundred yards, since the boats, though big enough to hold a couple of dozen people, had no means of propulsion besides their oars. The bright-eyed, quick-gestured oarsman on the boat in which I embarked showed me the calloused palms of his hands, whitish pink against the black skin.

"Why don't you get an outboard motor?" I said. "In Singapore, where I used to live, no one would think of rowing a boat like this."

"Yes, I would like to get a motor," he said. "But government does not allow. No permit."

"Ah, of course. You need an import permit."

"Cannot get without permit. Cannot get permit. So we row!"
He laughed.

In a few minutes we had passed under the stern of a Russian
freighter and were across. I walked up the slope to the road at the
top, where a pedicab man ran forward to hustle me into his tricycle.
I was reminded of old Malacca by the narrow street and the higgledy
piggledy warehouses, smelling of pepper, cardamom and other spices.

My man pedalled me over the canal and on to the northern end
of the island, which is the part that was formerly enclosed within
the walls of the fort. It had the same sort of history of relation-
ships with the outside world as Malacca too. To start with there
were the travellers' accounts from the fourteenth and fifteenth
centuries—Ibn Battuta, the Arab; Ma Huan, the Chinaman; and
Abdur Razak, the Persian. Then, in the first year of the sixteenth
century, the Portuguese arrived, after which it became their first
settlement in India.

Pedro Alvares Cabral, discovering the coast of Brazil, as it were
by mistake, on his way, arrived at Cochin in the year 1500, two
years after Da Gama had reached Calicut. He took on a cargo of
pepper and established a trading station, but this was only after he,
himself, had been to Calicut, where the trading post that the Moslem
ruler, the Zamorin, had allowed him to set up was burnt down by
his Arab rivals. In retaliation he destroyed ten of their ships and
bombarded the town.

Therefore, when two years later Da Gama landed at Cochin on
his second voyage, it was as a friend of the Raja of Cochin and an
enemy of the Zamorin of Calicut. The timely arrival of Albuquerque
just saved the little town from invasion by the Zamorin in 1503.
He built a wooden fort out of the trunks of coconut-trees bound
together by iron bands, and called it Fort Manuel after the King of
Portugal. In 1510 Albuquerque was made Viceroy in Cochin, and
in 1524 Vasco da Gama died there. In 1548 St Francis Xavier
stayed there, preaching and making converts to Christianity.

At the beginning of the next century Englishmen were offering
assistance to the Zamorin of Calicut in his attacks on Cochin in
return for permission to set up a factory there. But in the end they
got permission from the Portuguese without fighting. They traded
there for twenty-eight years until in 1663 the Dutch came on to the
scene, captured Cochin from the Portuguese and built a smaller,
stronger fort.

From all this century and a half of Portuguese occupation little remains, for the Dutch destroyed all the churches and convents except for one—the Church of Saint Francis—which they converted into a Protestant chapel. Built in 1510, it is the oldest church in India apart from the ancient holy places of the Syrians, and it is still in use, though much dilapidated, although it was restored in 1779 and again later. It is now classed as a protected monument.

I walked into this church past the bamboo ladder, which a couple of workmen had put up to plaster over holes in the façade. The roof was of corrugated iron, and stretched beneath it across the nave, were the long *punkas,* made of cloth, which were used in the old days as fans. There were cords leading from them through holes in the walls, so that they could be operated by slaves on the ground outside the church.

My man pedalled on through the quiet residential area of this old-style cantonment, until he came out on the northern shore, facing the entrance to the lagoon. Here there were some slight signs of activity, for along the foreshore, stretching from the wharf westwards, there was a row of contraptions made of bamboo, ropes and netting. Some were sticking up into the sky like giant spiders' webs, and others were dipped down into the water.

They were fishing nets of the Chinese type that can be seen at the ends of the long fences of the fish traps in the shallow waters round Singapore. But here, in Cochin, they were simply suspended from derricks of roped bamboo on platforms sticking out a few feet from the sea wall. The black fishermen wound the nets up and down, catching little or nothing, going through the motions they had been taught to make without the slightest thought of change.

A well-dressed man came running towards me. "How lucky you have come along," he said eagerly. "Please take a photograph."

"Well, it might make a good photograph," I said. "But the sun's in the wrong direction."

"Never mind about the sun. You *must* take a photograph. Let me have a copy quickly."

"What for?"

"Here. This is my card. You send it to me, please."

"Ah. Mr George."

A small crowd had gathered. Mr George called out to them to make way.

"But what's all the fuss about?" I said.

"The net. I must show the photograph to government, so that they can see the net. You see how it's torn to pieces?"

"Ah yes, I do now."

"The ship did it this morning, going into the jetty. The Samundar."

"Indian ship?"

"Oh yes. Indian ship, of course. Without a photograph I can get nothing."

"And how much do you expect to get?"

"One thousand rupees those nets cost. They must pay me one thousand rupees."

"Why don't you get a camera for yourself?"

"No permit."

"All right."

I took the photograph, pocketed Mr George's card, and climbed back into my pedicab. We went south again, past the modern Santa Cruz Cathedral and Vasco da Gama House, which is the bishop's residence, and along a straight road without any four-wheeled traffic on it, to a rectangular, cream-coloured, two-storeyed building, which is the second of the two Portuguese edifices that remain.

The Mattancherry Palace was built by the Portuguese for the Raja of Cochin. It still contains the panoply of royalty—the Masnad in the throne room, where coronations took place, and the palanquin with its golden canopy, standing under a fine, gleaming, chocolate-coloured roof, which is nowadays lit by neon lights—for this was not Goa, where the Portuguese held absolute sway and no native ruler remained. The Raja of Cochin retained his identity as a Hindu king, an ally rather than a puppet of the Portuguese.

The rich and sensuous paintings of the Hindu gods and goddesses are still there on the walls—Vishnu painted blue-black, with the great heads of the supernatural cobra forming a canopy above him; Siva embracing his wife, Parvati; Krishna surrounded by the Gopi girls; Lakshmi sitting on the lotus flower. At one time, after the Raja had moved to more spacious quarters, an attempt was made to whitewash some of them over, as they were thought to be obscene, but the work was stopped before much damage was done, and so they still remain to delight the connoisseur and intrigue the inquisitive.

The Dutch occupation lasted nearly as long as the Portuguese. But after 130 years the British took over, following their successful war against Tipu Sultan, whose father had subjugated the northern part of the state. They, in their turn, occupied the town for roughly the same length of time, and did as much damage as the Dutch had done, for orders were received from London to blow up all the fortifications and all the public buildings, including the fine offices of the Dutch East India Company. Meanwhile the Rajas continued as the titular rulers of the state, and in later generations sent portraits of themselves far and wide, with their heads wrapped in the symbolically knotted turban cloth, on the official postage stamps.

The Jews have been in Cochin longer than British, Dutch or Portuguese and after driving back into the narrow streets near the waterfront, I found their synagogue tucked away up a cul-de-sac. We knocked on the locked door to gain admittance. After a few minutes a woman came down from an upper room to let us in. Though dark and lined, she certainly had the beaked nose and lean features of the Semites. I apologized for disturbing her at a time when the synagogue was closed, but she was not put out and courteously opened up for me.

From the dark anteroom we moved into a square hall glittering with glassware in the shape of candelabra and lamp globes. The ark, bound in gleaming brass, stood on a floor of white Chinese tiles with the blue willow pattern on them, and the whole effect was one of startling light and richness in that mean alleyway.

The synagogue is 300 years old, for the original building was burnt down in 1662 in the struggles between the Portuguese and the Dutch, and the present building was put up two years later with assistance from the new masters. But of course, the Jews have been in Cochin far longer than that. According to their traditions they were trading with the Malabar coast as far back as King Solomon's time, and they founded a permanent settlement in Cochin after the destruction of the temple in Jerusalem in A.D. 70.

The Jews were formerly divided into the white and black sects according to their colour. Arguments arose as to whether the black Jews were of genuine Jewish race, having been blackened by living for many generations in the heat of the sun, or whether they were merely the descendants of slaves brought by the white Jews and converted by them to Judaism. The arguments occasionally broke out into actual riots, but they have worn thin enough today. Emigration to Israel and elsewhere has reduced this once flourishing community to no more than a few hundred souls.

I offered the Jewish lady caretaker some money for her trouble in coming down at midday to show me the old treasures—the fourth- or fifth-century copper plate, which records Raja Bhaskara Ravi Varma's grant of land for the synagogue; the great scrolls of the Books of the Law; and the reading desk—but she would accept none. Proud of her ancestry, she belied the money-seeking reputation of her race, and ushered me out as courteously as she had shown me in.

I went back in my pedicab to the jetty through streets that smelt so strongly of pepper that I started sneezing. The rowing boat was there just as I had left it hours before. The young oarsman, it seemed, had been waiting half the morning for me.

"No need to get an outboard motor," I said, "If there's nowhere else to go."

"I get an outboard, take you other places—Boghatty Island, Vallarpad Island, Vaipin Island. Very nice!"

"No, thank you. It's too hot."

"You help me get a permit for the motor, please."

"I'm sorry. I can't help you. You've got nowhere to go, so you'd better stick to rowing."

A large barge went slowly across our bows, deeply laden with copra, with a rough awning of matting amidships under which the bargee and his crew lived. It had a small sail up, but there was hardly a breath of wind, and it too was propelled simply by the power of human muscles. Two men poled it along through the shallow inshore water like an enormous punt.

Back at the Malabar Hotel everyone was settling down for the afternoon sleep, and even the crows were silent. After a late lunch I tried to sleep as well. But it was too hot, and a crow kept hopping in and out of the window in a pointless dance. It seemed strange that I was there at all. I went down to the swimming pool and lay in the water instead, finding myself the only person there. An Indian Navy Pinnace came up to the hotel's private jetty. The young sailors tied her up, the officer came ashore, sat for half an hour on the jetty doing nothing, then took his boat away again.

As the sun went down, the crows started up their cawing once more. I was invited into the bar by an American travel courier, driven to distraction by a dozen elderly women and three elderly men, who had paid $4,000 each to go sightseeing round the world. We stood facing an advertisement for the gin I remembered from wartime days—don't be wavered, ask for Hayward—whilst the barman went on with his task of squeezing limes into a jug. Customers had to wait patiently until he had finished, which, after all, was not unreasonable as they had nothing else to do.

"Don't mind the limes," the courier said. "Just give me the gin."

"Just give me the lime," I said.

"There was this factory we went to where they make coir mats," he said. "It was out on Gundu Island. And of course they were all interested in these mats. And the manager showed us around, and he explained everything, and he showed us how they take the coir off the coconuts and stretch out the threads of the coir and then weave it and bind it in with the yarn. And there was this Mrs Ruby L. Rosebaum saying, 'What did he say?' all the time. 'What did he say?' There's always one like that. So I told her. And she still kept on saying, 'What did he say? You tell me, Mr Wacker! So I said, 'Look, they're showing you too. Can't you see what they're doing?' 'No. I just can't quite make out what they really are doing,' she says. So in the end I tell her, 'Mrs Rosebaum,' I say. 'If you can't hear what he's saying, and you can't understand what I'm saying, and you can't see what they're doing either, then there's only one thing I can say. I guess you must have wasted your money to come on this gosh darned tour'."

"It's International Tourist year," I said. "Must be nice to tourists."

"I'll be nice to tourists tomorrow," he said. "That's my job. Right now I'll have another shot of that Hayward's gin."

I went into the dining-room, where Mrs Rosebaum and the other American tourists were having their meal, but the man I sat with was an Englishman. He had come down to Cochin from Bangalore to catch a P. and O. cargo-passenger ship for home. However, the ship, which was named the *Coromandel* after the Coromandel Coast on the eastern side of the peninsula, had not yet arrived.

"I went to the shipping office again today," he said. "And they still couldn't tell me when it's coming. 'Daily we are expecting it,' they said. 'No definite informations.' So here I am, still waiting."

"Are you going home for good this time?" I asked, looking at his ealn face and stiff, slow limbs, the result, I supposed, of a lifetime in the tropics.

"No. Not this time. Six months' leave, then back again, if my arteries can still stand it. So long as I can get around the golf course, and keep fit that way, I'll survive."

He was a man in holy orders, whose life's work was with the Protestant churches and schools of southern India, and age or ill-health or Indian independence were not going to stop him carrying on for as long as he had the ability to do so.

Next morning I looked out of my window through the crow screen, and saw the big ship passing up the channel to its dock on Willingdon Island, and I was pleased that the clergyman's wait was at an end. But I myself took another boat—the ferry that plies to and from the mainland, carrying the dockyard workers back and forth, and bringing the clerks who work in this, the last of the British cantonments, so recently reclaimed from the sea, in offices such as the Ministry of Finance, the Ministry of Health and Family Planning, and the Cantonment Enforcement Directorate.

I listened to the passengers talking in their Malayalam language, which sounds like water running through a pipe. But when I got to the ferry point at Ernakulam, English fell on my ears once again. A pedicab man hustled me away, thinking I was off an American ship on shore leave to have a "gay time". Rather disappointed at merely showing me the town, he pointed out the courts, the statue of the Raja, the collectorate, as the tax-collectors' offices are called in India, and the shops in the main street, which was called, of course, Mahatma Gandhi Road. I was expected to show pride in the U.S. destroyer that was on its way through the lagoon to the naval anchorage, and nothing I could say would persuade him that I was neither American nor a sailor.

I went back to the jetty to return to my island. Ernakulam seemed as quiet and somnolent as Cochin had done the day before. There was no new spirit of revolution in the air. There were no wall posters, no flags, no processions. The proletariat had yet to march with banners unfurled. If the Communists intended to inject a new dynamic into the state of Kerala, they had yet to stir the people of Cochin.

THE FISH-EYED GODDESS

I T IS a quarter past four in the morning, and for over twelve hours the train has been rumbling through the northern part of Kerala, over the hills in the centre of the peninsula and down into the flat country of the Tamils. We have entered an ancient land, with a history that goes back to the great days of Classical Greece in the fourth and fifth centuries before Christ.

The train stops. I stare up at the signs in my compartment: "Passengers are requested not to smoke if co-passengers object to smoking." "Please do not play radios if objected to by other passengers." Outside, on the wall of a loading bay, the motto, "Load one more ton in each waggon" is written in large white letters. From the other side, beyond the raised shutters of the carriage window, come the cries, "Cold drink! Roast milk!" raucous in the night.

Now that the bumping is over I settle down to sleep, but I am soon disturbed. My coach is to be shunted off into a siding, and I am turned out to seek refuge in the station retiring rooms. I claim the "rest room for foreign tourists", and the attendant shows me how to sleep on a couch, which looks as though it has found its way there from some nineteenth-century boudoir, with my feet propped up on a chair placed beside it. The Indian lying prostrate on the floor does not stir, nor does he do more than turn over with a groan, when I leave my resting place three hours later to go and look for breakfast.

It is a satisfying English breakfast of cornflakes, fried eggs, chips and potatoes, and enough strength returns to my limbs to go out into the open and find my way to the great pagoda half a mile away —the temple of the fish-eyed goddess of Madurai.

This temple, the foremost in southern India, is both ancient and modern. Although the greater part of it was built between the thirteenth and seventeenth centuries, its history goes back to the first stone building in the seventh century and to earlier shrines in brick and wood which stood on the same spot. Yet as recently as 1963 a complete renovation and redecoration was completed, which cost two million rupees. As I walked past three of the great towers above the gateways, with their myriad carved figures, freshly painted in reds, greens and blues, and made my way along the outer wall, with its screen of palms, to the main entrance and the grinning figures at the door, I felt that, at last, I had at least salvaged one reality out of the romantic imaginings that had existed in my youthful mind when I first sailed for India. The palms, the temple towers and the white-robed priests were all there, the worshippers were passing in and out, and what was more, this was not like the Great Pagoda of Jagganath at Puri. Provided one left one's shoes at the door and paid twenty-five paisa for someone to look after them, one could go inside.

I entered the hall of the eight *shaktis,* where shopkeepers sell food and sweets, bangles, toys and flower garlands, renting their places for forty rupees a month, below the eight goddesses sculptured on the big stone pillars, which support the roof. Sitting beside their multicoloured stalls in the cool shade, they reminded me of the money-changers Christ chased out of the temple in Jerusalem. But it cannot be said that they have no right to be there, for this hall and the one beyond it, guarded by two fearsome giant doorkeepers, though within the outer enclosure of the temple precincts, are not within the temple wall itself.

At the end of the second hall, which has over a hundred columns in it with capitals in the form of the banana flower and the strange *yalli,* which I first met at Vijayanagar, there is a large door of brass that at night gleams in the light of many lamps. One passes through the open doorway onto the long colonnades that surround the sacred pool. Even there one is only on the fringe, for the whole complex is like a set of Chinese boxes, one within another.

First there is the outer wall, and within it lie the tradesmen's halls, the pavilion of the bull, the hall of a thousand pillars that now houses an exhibition of Hindu metaphysics, and other smaller buildings. Then one comes to the inner wall, which encloses an area divided into three parts—the sacred pool, the temple of Siva, and the temple of the Fish-Eyed Goddess. Then within each temple there are yet more concentric walls until the actual shrine containing the image of the god or goddess is reached. Thus the pilgrim advances, passing through doorway after doorway, first purchasing his offerings, then bathing and cleansing himself, then making obeisance to the lesser deities, then carrying out the ritual, then advancing for the supreme moment, the actual view of the god or goddess as represented in the image. It reminded me, absurdly, of a striptease show, where each garment is removed one by one until nothing but the naked truth remains.

The pool is known as the Tank of the Golden Lily, and is oblong in shape, with a pillar in the centre surmounted by the flower from which it takes its name. Terraces lead down to the water, and worshippers walk down them to bathe and drink, whilst the walls at the back of the colonnades are set with pictures of the sixty-four most famous pagodas of India, and with marble slabs inscribed with all the stanzas of the Tirukkural.

The latter, called the "sacred couplets", are a beautiful collection of moral aphorisms in Tamil verse, said to have been written by the poet, Tiruvalluvar, not later than the fifth century A.D. They say that he wrote a thousand verses and presented them to the academy of the poets, but they were not accepted because they were in rhymes of three lines instead of rhymes of four. In disgust he threw them all into the pool, and out of them grew the golden lily that adorns it.

These lines could almost be called the Bible of the Tamils, for the thought is lofty, as in the following examples:

> For a kindness done without expecting reward
> heaven and earth are hardly enough recompense.

> The delight of the avenger lasts only a day
> The delight of the peacemaker lasts for ever.

> They who fast and do penance are great,
> But they who forgive wrongs are even greater.

And on a more mundane level the aphorisms are still sweet and kindly:

> Wide as the sea is the joy of love,
> but wider still the sorrow of parting.

> Vain is the kingdom where all good things exist,
> but no love between ruler and ruled.

(*right*) Mahabalipuram
—Descent of the Ganges
(*below*) Madras—
Mahatma Gandhi

Ajanta—(*above*) the caves. (*left*) Indian tourists

> Sweethearts delight in a lover's quarrel
> for the greater joy of making it up.

These are only a few examples of the whole work, and the work itself is only a fraction of the whole body of Tamil poetry, for the Tamil Nad, the Land of the Tamils, is, perhaps more than anywhere else, a land of poets. Their ancient history tells of poetical academies as much as of wars and battles, conquests and subject peoples. According to Nakkira there were three of these poetical Sanghams. The first, lasting 4,440 years, had 549 poets as members and published the works of 4,449 authors. The second lasted for 3,700 years and published the same number of authors, although it only had fifty-nine members. The third lasted 1,850 years and gave the works of 449 poets to the world.

These figures, as is the way in India, at first sight look very odd. But one must remember that the first two Sanghams were legendary, and that the places where they were located have long ago disappeared under the sea. Nevertheless the historical third Sangham, though it may not have lasted quite as long as Nakkira says, produced eight anthologies containing over 2,000 poems, attributed to more than 200 authors.

And this is not all. Yet up to fifty years ago this great body of literature, written in an archaic language, which the Tamils themselves find difficult to read, lay almost forgotten, and most of the rare manuscripts still remain to be edited and given to the modern world.

Standing in the eastern colonnade of the pool, I was able to watch the bathers going up and down the terraces, sprinkling water over their heads and filling their brass and silver pots with it. Above the colonnade on the far side, I could just see, amongst the higher towers of the gateways, the golden *vimanas* above the two shrines of Siva and his mate.

As these are the two hearts of the temple, it is of interest to know what their history is and what they contain. The larger of the two is the one that is dedicated to Siva, but the holy place is always known by the name of his wife, the fish-eyed goddess, Meenakshi Ammon. If one enters through the columned hall, where the shopkeepers now sit, and where formerly the temple elephants, camels and bulls were tethered, and along the northern colonnade of the pool, one comes in a direct line to the doorway of the shrine. The great gateway, with its 150-foot tower, that leads in a direct line to the door of Siva's shrine, is not so much used.

Parvati, the consort of Siva, is often known by the attributes of her eyes. In Benares she is broad-eyed. In Kanchipuram, near Madras, which Anglo-India knew as Conjeeveram, she is Kamakshi, Loving-Eyed. Here in Madurai her epithet, Meenakshi, calls to mind the elongated eyes that are beloved of Indian painters, rounded at the nose, but tapering away into tails curling up towards the temples. Meenakshi is, in fact, quite a common name for Hindu girls and is frequently shortened to the simple Meena.

It is related in the old legends, called the Puranas, that in the time of the Pandya kingdom, which was already flourishing when Asoka was Emperor of India, there was a king named Malayathuvasan, whose wife, Kanchanamala, was without child. In her previous birth she had been an ardent devotee of Parvati, and moved by her devotion, the goddess had appeared before her in the form of a young girl, and asked her what she most desired. She had replied that she would like Parvati to be born as her daughter in the same form as the one in which she now appeared.

Thus it was that, when Malayathuvasan and Kanchanamala were performing the appropriate rites, a three-year-old girl appeared out of the sacred fire and sat on Kanchanamala's lap. Malayathuvasan was disappointed. He had hoped for a son, and furthermore the girl who had come out of the fire, had three breasts. But God told him to bring the girl up as a boy, and that her third breast would disappear on first seeing the man who was to become her husband.

Consequently the king brought her up as a prince, and when she came of age, he named her as his successor and performed her coronation. The virgin queen embarked on a series of wars and defeated all the foes of the Pandyas. She even marched on Mount Kailas, the sacred abode of Siva in the Himalayas. There, at last, she met her match, for though she defeated Siva's warriors, when the god, himself, rode out on to the battlefield, she was transformed. Her third breast disappeared, and she stood rooted to the spot.

Eight days later Siva came to Madurai to marry her in a wedding ceremony that was celebrated with the utmost pomp and magnificence. He danced for the people and ruled the Pandyas as a mortal king. He still performed miracles, however, and after the son Kanchanamala had borne him had been crowned as his successor, he retired with her into the Great Temple, where they assumed their divine forms of Sundareshwar and Meenakshi Ammon.

This is the legend, and every April the marriage of Siva and Meenakshi is celebrated in memory of the original event. Here, too, the people come to perform their own mortal weddings. As I came to the altar in front of the Meenakshi Temple, I found a couple in the process of being married. The figure of Meenakshi looked plump and overdressed, swathed in ropes of pearls, whilst Siva was represented by a blue lingam with a face on it.

It was the pearls that sent my mind on another train of thought, for apart from the produce of a fruitful land, it was pearls that originally brought wealth to the courts of Madurai. Marco Polo came to the Tamil Nad in the late thirteenth century, at the very end of the long Pandyan rule. He calls India, as many of the old-time travellers did, the "noblest and richest country in the world", and describes the pearl fisheries of the coast below Madurai. He refers to the shark-charmers:

"In consequence of the gulf being infested with a kind of large fish," he says, "which often prove destructive to the divers, the merchants take the precaution of being accompanied by certain enchanters, belonging to a class of Brahmans, who by means of their diabolical art, have the power of constraining and stupefying these fish, so as to prevent them from doing mischief; and as the fishing takes place in the daytime only, they discontinue the effect of the charm in the evening, in order that dishonest persons who might be inclined to take the opportunity of diving at night and stealing the oysters, may be deterred by the apprehension they feel of the unrestrained ravages of these animals."

I thought I heard the romantic melodies of Bizet's opera, *Les Pêcheurs de Perles* as I looked at the ropes of pearls painted on Meenakshi's picture, and the temple official in his white dhoti and coloured sash, who came up to me at that moment, seemed to be the very image of Nourabad, the High Priest of Candi.

The Pandyas went down under the Moslem general sent by the Sultan of Delhi, and a period of half a century followed, during which, according to Ibn Battuta, the temples were closed and the people were oppressed. Nevertheless, the really great days of the Meenakshi temple were yet to come, for the Hindu revival in Vijayanagar extended to Madurai. The Vijayanagar general, who was sent to place the Pandya back on his throne, seized power for himself and founded the rule of the Nayaks, which lasted for 200 years.

During this time of Hindu revival, and particularly during the reign of Tirumala Nayak, the Great Temple was extensively renovated and its administration was reorganized. The last of the Nayak rulers was a woman. She was named Meenakshi after the goddess, and having no heir, she adopted a boy as her son. But the boy's father claimed power for himself, and sought help from the Nawab of Arcot, the neighbouring Moslem ruler. The Nawab's General, Chanda Sahib, promised help to both sides and gave it to neither. He chased the boy's father out of the country and imprisoned the virgin queen, who committed suicide in jail.

Thus the Muslims returned again. But they were not united, and the intervention of the British and French complicated the struggles for mastery, as one side backed one man and the other another. The situation was clarified when, fifty years later in 1780, Haidar Ali swept into the Tamil Nad from Mysore. The British fought him off, nominally assisting the Nawab, Mohammed Ali, but when he was eventually forced to retreat, they demanded compensation for their losses. The Nawab had no money, so he told the British to collect taxes from the people and reimburse themselves that way. And so George Procter, the first Collector of Madurai, arrived in 1781. In 1790 the British assumed power without any formalities, divided the country into districts and appointed a collector for each one. The whole of the Tamil Nad remained British from then on until 1947.

It was Tirumala Nayak, who built the surrounds to the Lake of the Golden Lily, and the great tower over the main entrance to the Siva Temple, or the Swami Koil, the Temple of the Husband, as it is called. He also set up the bronze doorkeepers of the Ammon Koil, which barred admittance to myself, a non-Hindu.

Meenakshi Ammon! The name, by a coincidence of sounds, brought to my mind another great shrine of the pagan world—the temple of Jupiter Ammon in the Oasis of Siwa in the Libyan desert, where the priests hailed Alexander the Great as the very son of the god. Nothing of that celebrated temple and oracle, described by Herodotus, now remains, but at Madurai the pagan rites and ritual continue to flourish unrestrained.

The temple official, who had attached himself to me as I watched the wedding party, explained how the groups of visitors are taken into the Ammon by the men wearing red sashes over their right shoulders and left hips, whom he called the temple peons, and then conducted into what he described as the *sanctum sanctorum*.

We could not follow into the holy of holies, where all the Nayaks used to be crowned, or see the bedroom and dining-room and other appurtenances of this gigantic house of the goddess, but we were able to see the people doing their *puja* in front of lesser idols, such as Ganesh, the elephant god, and the dancing Siva. They would place their hands together and jog up and down murmuring mantras. Nothing was organized except for the iron safes with holes cut in them for the money.

"The revenue of the temple is six lakhs of rupees (Rs 600,000) per annum," the Nambiar said. "It comes from rents and from the people doing puja and from philanthropists. The safes are opened in the temple treasury with everybody present, and the money is counted and deposited."

The revenue has therefore increased fifty fold from 1801, when the Collector of Madurai under the British administration first took control. The temple finances were handed back to the Hindus forty years later after Christian clergymen had agitated against Englishmen administering Hindu temples. Under the Hindu Religious and Charitable Endowments Act of 1959 the temple is now administered by a committee under the control of the Commissioner.

One of the most popular of the money-making safes was placed under the statues of two dancers, spattered with clarified butter by devotees. Siva had entered into a dance contest with a Devi. The Devi danced well, but Siva varied his dance by kicking his legs up. This the goddess could not do, because it would be too immodest for her, so Siva won.

Another safe constantly frequented by the Hindu worshippers stood below a stone table, on which were placed the symbols of the nine planets. Each devotee placed a little oil lamp in front of the one that accorded with his horoscope.

So we passed through the outer ambulatory of the Swami Koil, moving amongst pillars that could have been in ancient Babylon, in a dim, mysterious atmosphere of oil and sandalwood. We went on into another vast hall that contains nearly a thousand pillars, and reminded me of the halls of Persepolis as they might have been before Alexander fired the Persian palace.

This hall now contains a sort of exhibition of Hindu religion and the story of the temple. Like the flow charts in some kind of fantastic systems analysis, the diagrams show the bewildering proliferation of the Hindu gods, each with his *shakti*, or goddess, his written symbol (circle, triangle and so on), his illumination (sun, moon, firefly, etc), his noise (drum, cymbal...). One is for a medical man, another for a theological man, another for an administrator. The mind reels. Yet this is no museum of ancient lore. It is all new stuff, as modern as the temple renovation of 1960 to 1963 and the ceremonial rededication marking its completion, which the President of India was only prevented from attending by an illness.

I studied these things, and they seemed to have no end to them, like the endless twists and turns of modern psychoanalysis. A bright young man looked up at me suspiciously. "What did I think of it?" he seemed to say. "What do *you* think of it?" I wondered. "Do you really believe all this, or are you like a man who sometimes knows he is mad, but is incapable of altering his madness?"

I preferred, to these bewildering metaphysical charts, the homely folk tales also illustrated in the hall of a thousand pillars. There was the tale of Mr Peter, the Collector in 1812, who used to ride horseback round the outer wall of the temple precincts before going to his office. In this way he was claimed as a devotee of Meenakshi and affectionately known by the people as Peter, the Pandyan. One night, when he was asleep, there was a severe storm. A young girl came into his bedroom, woke him up and beckoned him outside. As soon as he had got out of the house, it was struck by lightning and destroyed. The little girl vanished, and Peter, convinced that the goddess, Meenakshi, had saved his life, presented a pair of golden, jewel-encrusted stirrups to the temple to be used on the horse that carried Meenakshi in procession.

I went out of the hall of a thousand pillars and left the temple area by the doorway that is surmounted by the massive Raya Gopuram. This great tower, which was built back in the thirteenth century, has over a thousand figures on it. All of them, together with the thousands of figures on the other three entrance towers, have been repaired and painted in bright colours by the renovators.

There was some argument about this, for there were people who followed the line popular amongst European savants and pedants, that it is pernicious to paint stonework, which is better left a dull grey like the ruins of Greece and Rome. But the painters won, and furthermore the people preferred the bright colours to pale pastel shades. So the voice of the people was heard, and I, for one, believe that they were right, for temples need bright colours to dazzle the eyes, and thus it was in Greece when her temples were still "live".

Forty thousand of the two million rupees were spent on the scaffolding alone for the repair of the towers, and people wondered how the money would ever be raised to complete the work. But the President of the Renovation Committee, Sri P. T. Rajan, used to pray to Meenakshi, saying, "If you want us to do this work, give us the means to do it, or we will leave it." And the money poured in, neither too much nor too little, until the work was done. It came from the general public and from business houses, exempted from income-tax by the Central Government, and from the surplus funds of other temples.

I left the Great Pagoda by the same doorway as I had used to go in, and walked back along the length of the temple walls to the road that leads away from the great gateway on the western side. It took me past a square tank, which was as large as the golden lily pool, but so dried up that there were only pools of water on the bottom of it. On the far side of it there stood a small church, as humble and modest as the temple was proud and magnificent.

It was the Roman Catholic church of Our Lady of the Rosary, and as I entered the low gateway of the compound from the rough track that lay between it and the tank, I heard the babel of high-pitched voices of children. They were in the crowded classrooms of the church school, being taught by Indian nuns. One of the nuns came out to me to ask me what I wanted, and to conduct me to the diocesan priest in his house on the other side of the church.

Father de Cruz had been the incumbent at Madurai for a year, and I put to him the question I had come to ask. Was this the church that the Italian Jesuit, Roberto de Nobili, founded when he came to Madurai to win souls and to try to convert Tirumala Nayak to his religion?

The Father was not sure. He thought the original church must have been either on this site or on the site of another, even smaller church now tucked away in a city street. But whichever it may have been, I liked to think of Nobili's house as having been on this spot.

For here his humble abode in a city, which even he, as a seventeenth-century Roman, regarded as beautiful, would have been in a direct line with the high towers of the temple that he wished to conquer.

It was an awe-inspiring ambition, as solemn and sublime, in its way, as that of the Jesuits in the Far East. For whilst the Portuguese had carved out enclaves for themselves on the coasts of India—in Goa, Cochin and the Pearl Fisheries—he was attempting to persuade the rulers of a great and ancient people of the interior to embrace the cross, whilst they were at the height of their magnificence and power.

Nobili was willing to go to great lengths to achieve this. Whilst more ordinary priests laboured amongst the simple people, giving absolution to fishermen and peasants, he went for the top. He put on the saffron robes of the Sannyasi, he accepted the Brahminical thread as being no bar to conversion, and he used his intellectual gifts and a deep knowledge of the Hindus, gained by profound study, to try to persuade the great men of Madurai of the truth of the Christian revelation.

When Nobili arrived in Madurai, Tirumala's father, Muthu-krishnappa, was still on the throne. His name, Muthu, means "The Pearl". On his death 400 wives joined him on the funeral pyre. It seemed fantastic and barbaric, but Nobili saw the event in another light. If only they could be converted to Christianity, a people with such a capacity for devotion and self-sacrifice would make noble and glorious martyrs for the faith.

Tirumala, himself, was thirty-nine when he came to the throne in 1623, but it was seven years before Nobili gained an interview, as a consequence of which he was given permission to preach and build churches in the state of Madurai. This was an achievement, but the Nayak was not really interested in Christianity. Surrounded by his courtiers, his 200 women and his elephants, he was mainly preoccupied with preserving his wealth against Vijayanagar to the north and the Portuguese in the pearl fisheries to the south. When he had to fight the Portuguese, Nobili and the other handful of Feringhees in Madurai were in peril.

Nobili laboured all his life in the Tamil Nad, and at times his influence became strong enough to disturb some of the Brahmins. But in the end it was the Muslims, not the Christians, who humbled the pride of the temple of Meenakshi Ammon. Perhaps Nobili's most striking success in that direction was his conversion of the master of the temple dancing-girls, whom he persuaded to sing in praise of Christ and the Virgin Mary instead of Siva Sundareshwar.

And so the ritual of the marriage of Swami and Ammon, in the month of Chait before the great rains come, continued to be celebrated year by year. Though there were many converts to Christianity in the Tamil Nad during subsequent centuries, when Christianity was the religion of the masters, Siva and Meenakshi never lost their power. And now that the Christians have handed over their mastery, a resurgence of Hinduism brings added impetus to the ancient rites. The age of the Nayaks is regarded as the golden age of the Tamil land.

This upsurge of Hinduism is seen in many forms, but perhaps it is at its most striking in the Institute for Rewriting Indian History. In their zeal to promote the Hindu cause learned members of this institute resort to tub-thumping language that verges on the ludicrous in describing the perfidy of their historical enemies. They plead for the renaming of cities that bear Moslem names like Allahabad and Ahmedabad, and they relate the tales of Moslem destructiveness and rape with grim satisfaction. The President of the Institute, in an article in *Mother India,* describes Mohammed Bakhtiyar of Bengal as "cracking down on the ancient Indian universities with hammer and tongs, torch and sword, axe and crowbar and chisel and spear".

Of course there is a certain truth in what he says, when he writes of the same Moslem chief as belonging to "that serried and solid phalanx of Moslem invaders who, like countless despicable termites, made short work of books, scriptures and Hindu seats of learning". On the other hand the technique of sweeping generalizations, unworthy of any institute of learning, becomes readily apparent when he goes from the particular to the general with the words, "If rape, rapine, treachery, falsehood, massacre, faithlessness, arson, larceny and devastation is civilization, then indeed the Muslims all over the world must be certainly credited with being real pioneers and avant-garde of a new civilization." Such writers are propagandists, not serious historians.

A truer spirit of Hinduism can be seen in the story of the *bhakti* movement, of those who followed the cult of intense personal devotion to the god or goddess of their choice. And perhaps the most devoted of all was Meerabai, who threw herself into an ecstasy of song and dance for her beloved Krishna. Yet the *bhakti* of the sixteenth century drew inspiration from the Sufis of Islam, of the religion that the "rewriters" of Indian history detest and despise.

Beloved, I wander still in quest of Thee.
I am athirst for thy eternal love.
I long to make my body a lamp,
The wick whereof will be my tender heart.
And I would fill the lamp with the scented oil
Of my humble love for Thee!
Then let it burn day and night
At they shrine, beloved Krishna.
I can no longer bear to be away from Thee.
Make me Thine own, make me like Thee,
And make me pure as Thou art, Beloved.

Nobili would have admired such devotion, albeit to Lord Krishna instead of to Jesus Christ.

I left the little church and went to visit Tirumala's old palace, a place of large, lofty pillars, supporting carved arches and ceilings, which is now used for the courts and government offices. Pleaders and scribes thronged the open-air galleries, and policemen in tall red turbans and khaki shirts and shorts kept some semblance of order. In the courtyard there were as many cars as I had seen in the whole of the town.

From this place I went back to the station. It was late afternoon. Thousands of schoolchildren were coming out of the compound of another, larger Catholic church, free from their lessons and wanting to have their photographs taken. By the time I had left them, two beggars, a boy and a girl, had latched on to me. They followed me down the street, alternately whining and ordering me to pay. The food shops were closing down, and sweepers were sweeping up the unsold rice on the pavements, covering it with clouds of dust.

An ice-cream vendor cycled past, with a pith helmet on his head and the legend, "Stop me and buy one" on his tricycle. At the T junction the road sign said simply, "Stop and Go". A cow lifted its tail. A woman blessed it with the palms of her hands together, then ran forward with the same hands cupped to collect the warm cowpats as they dropped. The scene was so familiar it might have been anywhere from Mathura to Madurai.

11

DOUBTING THOMAS

"BECAUSE THOU hast seen me, Thomas, thou hast believed; blessed are they that have not seen and have believed."

As I read these words in Latin, they seemed to be directed at me, for I myself, had not made up my mind whether to believe or disbelieve.

I was in a low cavern not more than sixteen feet square, which would have been as dark as night, if it had not been for the electric light, since the entrance was a mere crevice and the only other natural light came in by a rough hole at the other end. The floor of the cave sloped gently towards the statue of Saint Thomas, which stood above the inscribed scroll—he to whom Jesus said, "Let me have thy finger; see, here are my hands. Let me have thy hand; put it into my side. Cease thy doubting and believe."

And why not believe? The tradition is that this was the very cave where Saint Thomas, the apostle, surnamed Didymus, the twin, sought refuge from the Brahminical officials who wanted to do away with him, and lived a simple, hermit-like existence. Near the cave stands a rough cross, chiselled on stone, in front of which the apostle is said to have spent long hours in prayer and meditation, whilst beside the cross, beneath a circular stone building, which acts as a canopy, a perennial spring flows out of the ground. The people say that the apostle, in order to assuage the thirst of the crowds who came to hear him preach, wielded his stick as Moses used his staff, and caused the water to gush out by striking the rock.

Amidst these ancient things there now stands a small, white church with two broad flights of steps leading up to it. It was built by a Portuguese in 1612 in honour of Saint Thomas, for the tradition was as strong as ever when the first of the Fidalgos came there. From the steps one looks down on the seashore of the Coromandel coast and on to the city of Madras. It is called the Little Mount—the Chinna Malai in Tamil.

There is really no strong reason why Saint Thomas should not have come here. The route between the Roman world and India, which was Rome's source for large quantities of fine muslins, pearls and spices, was well established. So it was no more difficult to travel from Palestine to India than to Greece or Rome. It simply took longer.

In fact, the course of Saint Thomas' travels as a missionary in South India has been plotted by ancient tradition. He landed, we are told, in A.D. 52 on Azhikode Island, which is separated from the mainland by the Malabar backwaters. A church at Cranganore, just north of Cochin, marks the spot. He founded six more churches in Kerala, and then went over to the east coast of the peninsula either by sea or by the well-frequented land route via Coimbatore.

It may seem strange to think of Christians living in India as long ago as they did in Asia Minor and Europe. One thinks of the sequence of religions in India as being Hindu, then Moslem, and then Christian, the latter two following the flag of the conquerors. But the story of Saint Thomas is well established. Long before the Nestorian Christians went to Malabar from Syria, there were Nazarani, as they were called, living there. In the year 190 the Bishop of Alexandria received a letter from them requesting him to send them a religious teacher, and in the fourth century both St Gregory Nazienzene and St John Chrysostom refer to Thomas as the apostle who went to India. St Ephraim, in one of his Syriac hymns, refers to his martyrdom, and to the eventual removal of his body to Syria.

> The devil was howling: "The Apostle, whom I put to death in India has followed me to Edessa. The power that is concealed in the tomb of Thomas tortures me."

Clearly the Christian fathers never doubted. The Venerable Bede talks of Peter, who received for share Rome; Andrew, Achaia (i.e. Greece) and Thomas, India. In the ninth century Alfred the Great of England sent Bishop Sighelm "beyond the seas to Rome and to St Thomas in India". Marco Polo refers to "the body of the glorious martyr, St Thomas the Apostle", and the "vast number both of Christians and Saracens" making the pilgrimage to his tomb, and taking away with them the red earth from the spot where he was killed.

But now we are anticipating, for the place where St Thomas is said to have actually died is on the top of another hill two miles away, called the Peria Malai, the Big Mount. Though it is only 300 feet high, it looks large enough in the surrounding plain. As St Thomas dragged his bleeding body up it, it must have seemed as high as a mountain.

Tradition varies as to the manner of his death. Mar Solomon, the thirteenth-century Metropolitan of Basra, says the king of the Indians stabbed him with a spear, because he baptized his daughter. Yet in the same century Marco Polo, the Venetian, avers that he was killed by accident. "Having retired to a hermitage, he was engaged in prayer and surrounded by a number of pea-fowls, with which bird the country abounds. An idolater, who happened to be passing that way, and did not see the holy man, shot an arrow at a peacock, which struck the apostle in the side."

From the hermitage on the Little Mount St Thomas dragged himself up the Big Mount to die. At that time there would have been no more than a rough track through the trees and bushes to the top. Now a flight of 135 steps, flanked by a double wall, makes the ascent of the bare hillside easy.

The tradition that states that St Thomas was killed by his enemies rather than by accident, maintains that the Indian king's men administered the *coup de grâce* with a lance on this spot, and the link with the past was confirmed when an ancient cross was discovered whilst the Portuguese were digging the foundations for the church they built there.

This cross, with dumbell extremities, was turned up accidentally by the workmen as it lay face downwards on a rough block of stone. A bird, touching the top of the cross with its beak, may represent the coming of the Holy Ghost, and though scholars differ widely as to the meaning of the inscription, they are all agreed that it does not date later than the fifth century, and is in the old Pahlevi language of Persia in the Sassanian period. It is similar to the crosses in three of the old churches of Malabar, and the language of the inscription would point to Nestorian influence.

The cross now stands on the main altar of the church, and many miracles have been ascribed to it. There was said to have been a streak of blood on it when it was found, and in the days of the

Portuguese power it was reputed to sweat moisture at certain times. Even the doubting Thomases were convinced that something extraordinary was occurring. But with the decline of Portuguese power the sweating ceased. The doubting Thomases raised their voices once again.

The doubters will also question the authenticity of the picture of the Virgin and Child, which occupies pride of place on the altar in front of the cross. It is said to be one of the seven painted by St Luke and to have been brought by St Thomas. In spite of its age the colours are still bright. The blue cloak, with its golden hem, and the purple edge of the inner hood contrast with the red of the Virgin's dress and the pale colour of her flesh.

As from the Little Mount, one looks out from the Big Mount across the flat land to the long, white line of the seashore and to the city sprawling back from it. But at the time of these events not even Fort St George, the original core of the city, existed. The next episode in the story of the wounding, death and burial of St Thomas takes place in the southern suburb five miles away, which one can see on the other side of the Adyar river. This is where the town of Mylapur, the "City of Peacocks", was situated in St Thomas' day, and where the apostle was buried close to the sea.

I went down there to follow the story through, and found a rather unattractive building in nineteenth-century Gothic standing almost on the seashore. It was the cathedral of San Thomé, built in 1893 in place of the original Portuguese church of the sixteenth century. I walked up the nave of the cathedral under the Gothic archway, with its inscription in English, "Thomas, one of the twelve, who is called Didymus." Then I came to a brass railing round an oblong pit in the transept. This pit, faced with marble, leads up to the excavation under the high altar, which is where the saint is said to have been buried.

Doubting Thomases have maintained that the whole thing was an invention of the Portuguese. But it was the tradition of the saint that led them to the spot, not the Portuguese who brought the legend of the saint there. Long before Vasco da Gama reached India, an old church existed there, and the place was known by the Arab sailors as Beth Thuma. When the Portuguese in Goa heard of it, the Viceroy ordered an investigation.

A certain Diogo Fernandes arrived at Beth Thuma with some

Armenians in 1517. He found a ruined chapel with a monument to the apostle, tended by an Indian, whose duty it was to keep a lamp burning in the holy shrine. He was shown the grave and also a footprint and a kneeprint.

Six years later, during the course of reconstructing the chapel, the Father who had been put in charge of the repairs, decided to open the grave. He received the approval of Manuel di Faria, Captain of the Fishery and Coromandel coasts, and with the help of Diogo Fernandes and others, he set to work.

They dug for two days to a depth of over ten feet down the side wall of the chapel, before they came to the tombstone. Under it they found some fragments of bones from the skull and spine, and a spearhead stuck on a short piece of a wooden shaft. These fragments are now contained in a jewelled reliquary in the custody of the prior of the cathedral. They also found a large earthenware pot, filled with earth, which they supposed to have been brought down from the Big Mount soaked in the apostle's blood.

The depth of the grave below the level of the surrounding land is an indication of its antiquity. But, of course, there was no body, the reason being that the principal remains had been taken to Edessa long before the Syrian Christians. Nevertheless the spot became a particularly hallowed one. Pope Paul V founded the Diocese of St Thomas of Mylapur, and the church became a cathedral. In recognition of the monastery founded there by the Augustinians to take charge of the grave, the bishop is still known as the prior.

It was because the celebrated shrine of St Thomas lay on the eastern seaboard of India that Camoens repeated the legend of the apostle's martyrdom in the Lusiads. He also tells the story of how the local Indian king was converted to Christianity. The High Priest of the Brahmins, in order to dispose of Thomas, killed his own son, and then accused the saint of the murder. Thomas brought the boy back to life, and the boy revealed the truth. The king was so impressed that he asked to be baptized there and then.

So the legend survives in the hot air of the new cathedral, which in that steamy climate already looks shabby after only seventy years. I looked at a memorial stone let into the floor, interested by the combination of Christian and Indian names: "Shri Anaparambil Joseph John, born in Kerala in 1893, Governor of Madras 1956, died 1957." Then I walked out into the sandy compound, within range of the roar of the surf, which was out of sight over the ridge of the foreshore. A little girl ran up to me, begging as though her life depended on it, and when I gave her something she ran off happily to buy a sweet.

I thought I had seen it all, and in a sense I had, for the remainder of the story takes place overseas beyond the roaring surf. Some time in the third century a Syrian merchant, named Habban, took the bones of the apostle home to Edessa with him. They remained there for nearly 900 years. Then they were moved once again to save them from the Turks, and taken to the island of Chios in the Aegean Sea.

The remains stayed in Chios for over 100 years, till once again they were moved westwards to prevent them falling into the hands of the Turks. This time it was to Ortona, a small port in Italy on the Adriatic coast opposite Rome. There they were deposited in the cathedral, but in 1943 they were again in danger, for the cathedral was blown up by the Germans. The relics, contained in a large silver bust of the apostle, were hidden away, walled up in the building, and were again providentially preserved to be replaced under the high altar in due course.

It seemed a far cry from the Coromandel coast to the allied armies battling their way up the leg of Italy, but it is in these devious ways that history moves, making the whole world kin. I walked up the sandy ridge, and looked out across the beach and over that sea, which other allied armies had crossed to take South-east Asia back from the Japanese. Then I took a pedicab and rode northwards along the straight Marina, which is the pride of Madras, running alongside the broad band of silvery sand.

The statues that I saw on the way brought me back from past history into the modern age, for I went past Gandhi, the little, bent, bald man with the little bent stick, and past the two sages of South India, Swami Vivekananda and Mrs Annie Besant. Perhaps it was the perpetual peace that followed the consolidation of the British administration, which made it inevitable for the heroes of Madras to be spiritual rather than military leaders.

At the beginning of this century Mrs Besant's Theosophical Society, founded in Madras, soon had a world-wide appeal. The fine concept of combining the noblest ideals of all religions in a single theme, uniting all mankind, was bound to capture the minds of those to whom at that time universal progress seemed to be man's destiny.

The theosophists have carried on in spite of the blunting of the original optimism in the trauma of two world wars. So have the followers of the Swami, who sought to free Hinduism from the trammels of ignorance and superstition, setting up the Rama-krishna mission in honour of the Hindu Saint of Bengal, who went back to the ancient Vedas for his inspiration. The Vedantists of the Ramakrishna Mission expressed themselves in good works like the Christian missionaries, striving in educational and medical as well as spiritual fields.

The torch of spiritual regeneration has continued to burn in the South in the Ashram of Sri Aurobindo Gose in Pondicherry, and in the teaching of Ramana Maharshi of Ernakulam. Vedanta has also crossed the Pacific to join the multitudinous sects of California, and today nobody raises his eyebrows in South India at the sight of a white man or woman in sandals and a saffron robe, not donning the dress of the Sannyasi, as Nobili did in Madurai, in order to mix more easily amongst those whose souls he wanted to win for Christ, but wearing it as the apt garb in which to drink at the fountain of Hindu philosophy and oriental wisdom and heal their own souls.

But when I first went to India, this was not so. When Maud Macarthy went out to the Himalayas and set up her ashram, in obedience to the mystic advisers, whom she called the Brothers, a host of curious Indians came to visit her and her spiritualistic medium, but she remained taboo to the British. It must have seemed extraordinarily strange to the administrators that she, who had been a violin virtuoso in London, should give up a promising life in the West to go out East and live in poverty with the cockney boy, through whom her familiar spirits spoke.

After a few years Maud Macarthy became Swami Omananda Puri, perhaps the first European woman ever to become an Indian sannyasi, and donned the saffron robe, which she still wore on her return to England right up to her death in 1967. As well as passing on the teachings of the Brothers, she delved deep into the mysteries of the Tantras and Tantric Yoga.

She has described how she, herself, felt the power called Kunda-lini, that is conceived of as a serpent coiled up at the base of the spine. The psychic power apparently resides in an occult centre

12

in the lower stomach, thought of as a *chakra,* or wheel. It rises up the spine into the other five chakras—in the throat, the frontal centre between the eyebrows, sometimes referred to as the "third eye", and other parts of the body.

Swami Omananda Puri felt the Kundalini surging up through her so powerfully that it seemed to be a danger that must be stopped. And so the Kundalini became dormant once again. As one reads the weird literature of the tantric magicians, one thinks that this may, indeed, have been just as well, for to the uninitiated it seems like pure gibberish.

The Muladhara Chakra, the wheel of the lower stomach, is conceived in diagramatic form as an open lotus flower with four petals. Each petal contains a syllable of the mystic chant —Vam sam sham sam. The *shakti,* or female power, presiding over this flower is Dakini and the god is Brahma, who is the aspect of shakti in her play of creation. A circle unites the four petals, and contains a square, coloured yellow to symbolize the earth. The square contains the "root letter" *lam* on its vehicle, the elephant. Under the arch of the *lam* reside the genital organs—the triangle standing on its point, called the Tripura, which symbolizes the female, and within it the "self-born" lingam in the shape of the male. The Kundalini serpent is coiled round the lingam, and has its head poised over the orifice of the River Sushumna.

This fantastic occult anatomy is the basis of the theory of Kunda-lini, the serpent power, and Shakti, the female power, the Earth Mother, the source of everything. The Tantra-Tattva subordinates all the gods and goddesses to Shakti. "Brahma", it says, "is her play of creation, Vishnu is the aspect of Shakti in her play of preservation, and Maheshwar (Siva) in her play of destruction. Surya (the sun) is the aspect of Shakti in her play as light and heat, Ganesh in her play as success. Radha, Lakshmi, Saraswati, Savitri, Durga, Sita, Rukmini and others are aspects of Shakti in her play as the Great Shakti who is the root of all shaktis, and in whom they all rest."

And of the doubters the Tantra has this to say: "Is he not the great grandfather of all sceptics who finds it in him to say that Shakti does not exist? What can be greater folly than that you, Oh Jiva (gross matter) should proceed to discuss the existence or non-existence of the Shakti, whose greatness is preached by Bhagwan (God), and whose greatness is such that Bhagwan has ordained that the name of Shakti should be uttered first, and then that of the possessor of shakti, declaring that he who shall fail to utter the names as Radha-Krishna, Lakshmi-Narayan, Uma-Maheshwar, Gauri-Shankar and Sita-Ram is guilty of a sin as great as that of murdering a Brahmin?"

The female is thus placed first. The shakti unites with the god in an act of sexual union, which has the effect of liberating the gross matter. The equally weird Mahakala Tantra explains another strange principle—that of the right hand and the left hand, the Purusha and the Shakti, the male and the female. So long as the right and the left remain equally strong, the bondage of this world endures. But when, by means of intense meditation, the shakti has been awakened and has overpowered the right, and has lost herself in gracious joy on his body, then she, who is bliss unalloyed, grants the highest liberation to Jiva. "For this reason the Mother, the saviour of the three worlds, is called Dakshina Kali."

In regions where tantrism still flourishes, such as Bengal and Nepal, they still make the images in stone and bronze showing the sexual union of the shakti and the god. But as for me, I beg leave to be a "great grandfather of all sceptics" and doubting Thomases. Nor did Swami Omananda Puri pursue the path of tantric magic further. She remained in India, listening to the voices of the spirits, which came to her through the medium of the Londoner, whom she still called the Boy, even when he was well past middle age. They went to Kashmir, to Benares, to Dehra Dun, to Bombay, to Calcutta, always on the move, not caring where they slept, accepting everything as a sannyasi should, sometimes in hovels, sometimes in palaces. They lived through the slaughters of the partition days, and they gave out the observations of the spirits concerning a multitude of subjects, including the political future of India, science, religion and the destiny of man. It was not until the Boy died in 1956 that the Swami returned to England.

When I got to the end of the Marina, crossed the Cooum river and went into Fort St George, I felt that I was on firmer ground, more familiar to me than that of the swamis and sannyasis, and more akin to that of the Indian Army officer I knew, who gained one for a mother-in-law. Was it nostalgia for the past that made the jemadar at the old gateway salute me, even though I was dressed in civilian clothes? Or was the fort, though occupied by Indian government offices, still regarded as the historical stronghold of the Europeans, who were still worthy of honour as they entered?

The gate I entered was one of three on the landward side. From it I went past the old barracks, and the modest houses that Clive and the Duke of Wellington occupied when they lived there, to the sea gate. Originally, when the fort was built about a century after the Portuguese went to investigate St Thomas' grave at Mylapur, one could pass directly through this gate to a waiting boat. But now the sea has receded so far that it is nearly a quarter of a mile away, and the walls themselves have sunk so far that, seen from inside the fort, they are not much higher than a balustrade, as ineffective as the old guns that ornament them.

Near this gate, across the shady car park for visitors to the Secretariat, stands St Mary's, the oldest English church in India. As I looked at it, a wave of homesickness swept across me, for it looked so very much like a church at home, with a tower in the classical style, similar to those of Christopher Wren's seventeenth-century London. The trees around it were of a bushy kind, without a palm to be seen, so that by exercising a small flight of fancy, one could imagine it in one of London's lesser city squares, standing behind its railings.

This is, no doubt, how its builders imagined it too, for Lockyer, going to divine service twenty-three years after it was consecrated, describes it as "inferior to the churches of London in nothing but bells, there being only one to remind sinners of devotion." Yet it was built without help from London, entirely on the initiative of the governor and servants of the East India Company, who lived in Fort St George, when the chapel they had became inadequate for the increasing population.

Subscriptions were raised from amongst the Protestant inhabitants of Madras, and one of the donors was Elihu Yale, then a "writer" and later governor, whose subsequent donation of funds for a college library in America resulted in one of the most famous universities in the U.S.A. being named after him. Then an architect was needed, so the master gunner of the fort was given the task.

Next, after the building of the church, came the question of consecration, as there was no bishop available, so they sought authority from the Bishop of London to depute their chaplain to carry out the ceremony. They bound themselves not to use the church for any other purpose than for Christian worship, and they also promised that, "We and our successors in this place will from time to time and ever hereafter as need shall be, so far as in us lies, see it conveniently repaired and decently furnished in such sort as a church ought to be."

This promise has been kept. After the city of Madras had expanded far and wide beyond the bounds of the fort, and other churches, including the cathedral, had been built, St Mary's became the garrison church. It remained so until August 1947, when the last British troops, the 1st Battalion the Essex Regiment, left, handing over to the 3rd Sikh Light Infantry. At the same time ecclesiastical affairs ceased to be a government responsibility, and the church was handed over to the Indian Church Trustees. But the Protestant citizens of Madras, exhorted to continue to fulfil the original promise of Governor Streynsham Master, continued to maintain it, and although it is now classed as a protected monument, it is still used for worship.

I walked into the church under the fans on their long suspension poles in the nave and the regimental colours laid up in the choir. Facing me above the altar was the big picture of the last supper, which is said to have been loot from the French when the British captured Pondicherry in 1761. Nearly 300 years of history are commemorated in this building. Governors, soldiers and civil servants have their monuments there. But the largest monument of all is in memory of a missionary, who was not even British.

Father Schwartz was sent to India by the Danish Government, and then supported by the English Society for the Promotion of Christian Knowledge. He travelled widely in South India in the troubled times of the eighteenth century, and his transparent honesty and goodness earned him such trust on both sides that, on several occasions, he acted as intermediary between the Company's government in Madras and the upstart Haidar Ali in Mysore. The monument shows him on his death bed in 1798, taking farewell of the orphans he had adopted, who included the Raja of Tanjore.

The epitaph on the memorial tablet reads as follows:

The late Hyder Ally Cawn, in the midst of a bloody and vindictive war with the Carnatic, sent orders to his officers to permit the Venerable Father Schwartz to pass unmolested, and shew him respect and kindness, "For he is a holy man and means no harm to my government."

The late Tuljajee, Rajah of Tanjour, when on his death-bed, desired to entrust to his protecting care his adopted son, Serfojee, the present Rajah, with the Administration of all Affairs of his Country.

The East India Company, anxious to perpetuate the Memory of such transcendent Worth, and gratefully sensible of the Public Benefits which resulted from its Influence, caused this Monument to be erected Ann. Dom. 1807.

Another tablet is written in the majestic prose of the Augustan age:

To the memory of Josiah Webbe Esq. For many years Chief Secretary to the Govt of Madras, and afterwards Resident at the Court of Scindia, where he died, the 9th of November 1804, aged 37 years. His mind, by nature firm, lofty, energetic, was formed by classic study to a tone of independence and patriotism not unworthy of the best days of Greece and Rome.

On the tablet a military officer, a civil servant, a Mohammedan and a Hindu mourn over a portrait medallion of the deceased. Many others commemorate those who died in India too soon to take the long voyage home. The later ones, after St Mary's became the garrison church, are all of army men—colonels and majors, lieutenants and ensigns, corporals, fusiliers and drummer boys; dead of wounds, of accidents, of sickness, of sunstroke; in Madras, in Bangalore, in Ootacamund, in Burma, in Penang, at sea. Now they are all gone, and no more tablets will be made for them. But the church is still open for all who will to go in and read.

I left the fort and went back to the hotel near the station, to which I had been recommended. It was old and run down, and presumably dated back as far as the great queen after whom it was named, though I had not thought about that when I went to book in. Another hotel, still in the hands of the builders, towered above it. Even its name sign had disappeared, as if it wished to run away and hide, and for some odd reason, as in a military barracks, a notice in my room gave its specifications, "17' 6" × 17' 6", 1 person."

It was absurdly cheap, and yet the service was genial and the food adequate. As I sat in the dining-room, gulping iced fresh lime whilst waiting for dinner to be served, I looked up at the Indian families wandering about in their slow, aimless way, and I wondered how many English families, in the last hundred years, had walked across from the station as I had done, and gone up to the rooms hired according to their dimensions. Soldiers, administrators, merchants, missionaries, they were a stream that had seemed endless once.

And still it is not quite ended. A spry old man came in, accompanied by a much younger man and woman, darted a few glances around, and came to join me at my table to make welcome company. He was a member of a select missionary order, called the Brethren, who number all told only about 1,500, of whom 800 are in India. He told me he had a small church in a silk-weaving town in the Tamil Nad, with twenty-five out-stations, and he had laboured there all his life, except for the home leave every five years.

I thought of the Apostle Thomas in Mylapur, of Nobili in Madurai, and of the man catching his boat home in Cochin. And still they come, these drops in the ocean of the East, determined and persistent, bringing a little comfort to the vast miseries of the poor, sometimes getting into trouble and accused of interfering in politics, as with the Naga war of independence, or of using starvation to make converts, as in Bihar, but in the main left unmolested by the Hindus.

The young couple were the latest recruits, having flown down from Bombay with their mentor in the Caravelle. They were simple people from Surrey, who felt they had the call, and they were still impressed by the luxury of the flight. They seemed very matter of fact for folk at the beginning of a great adventure, being mostly concerned with the practical domestic problems of living in India and the question of servants. But perhaps that was just as well. The practical people are the ones that stay the course. I only hoped they would not be too patronizing to the poor Indians they had come to save.

Next morning the man from Topaz Travels came to take me on another excursion to that old India, which flourished between the coming of St Thomas and the arrival of the Portuguese. The broad, straight Mount Road, which is one of the main thoroughfares of Madras, was no longer hot and crowded, as it had been the day before, and it only took a few minutes to reach the foot of the Big Mount. We drove on, through the early morning, over the Adyar river, and across an empty, sandy plain, screened from the sea by bushy tamarisk trees.

After about an hour we turned into a tongue of land between a canal and the sea, and then went left towards a ridge of granite outcrops by the shore. Close to the ridge we came to a small village, where we stopped.

This was the place that has been known for centuries as the site of the Seven Pagodas. Now there are only two, for, as at Mylapur, the sea has been gradually eating away the land along this shore, and five of them, we are told, have been washed away by the sea. It is highly probable, for even the remaining two have had to be protected by a modern sea wall, built in 1954, which embraces the eighteen-foot stump of the ancient lighthouse, that used to be seventy-five feet from the shore. There was obviously a town of some size here, for it was probably the port for Kanchipuram, the capital of the Pallavas. Its name, Mahabalipuram, means the city of great Bali, and the mass of carvings and rock reliefs in the neighbourhood, together with the story of the sunken temples, inspired Southey in writing "The Curse of Kehama".

> The sepulchres
> Of ancient kings, which Bali in his power
> Made in primeval times, and built above them
> A city like the cities of the gods—
> Being like a god himself. For many an age
> Hath Ocean warred against his palaces,
> Till overwhelmed beneath the waves—
> Not overthrown—so well the awful chief
> Had laid their deep foundations.

Nothing now appears above the waves, and the line of breakers, under which the five pagodas are supposed to lie, looks too far away to be likely to conceal them. More probably they are closer at hand than the foam-flecked reef a mile out to sea. On the other hand, it would not have been beyond the wit of a talented people to erect buildings on the reef, both as a landmark and a breakwater. No one knows for certain, and no one will know until skin diving catches on in Madras and someone thinks it worth his while to explore the sea bed in the region of the two remaining pagodas.

I walked over the sand to these two, and found that they were really one, the smaller tower being simply the porch to the larger. It all looked very ancient, weathered by the salt spray and beaten by the sea. Siva's bulls were worn away almost beyond recognition, and the large reclining figure, which is supposed to represent Bali himself, is so eroded that it looks like a primitive image.

Yet the shore temple is probably the most modern of the antiquities of Mahabalipuram. According to the old legend Bali was a wise king, but too ambitious. He decided to enlarge his kingdom, and with this in mind, he performed a great sacrifice, which was so prodigious that it won him the kingdom of the gods. Vishnu, the Preserver, had at that time been unwilling to intervene, but later the gods managed to propitiate him with penances and prayers, and in consequence he came to earth as a deformed dwarf, named Vamana.

The dwarf went begging to Bali, and the latter, who was famous for his generosity, asked him to say what he wanted. The dwarf replied that he only wanted as much land as he could bestride in three paces. Naturally enough Bali promised to comply with so small a request. Thereupon the dwarf suddenly grew to such a fantastic size that he covered the three worlds in only two paces. Bali not only lost his kingdom, but as he had no more land to give the transformed dwarf for his third pace, he was sent to the nether regions for being unable to keep his promise. However, his subjects loved him so much that they begged Vishnu to allow him to visit his lost kingdom once a year, and Vishnu agreed. So Bali, who may have been a real Dravidian king, overcome by the Aryans, was welcomed back annually all over South India with feasting and merry-making at the festival of Onam.

Some scholars, on the evidence of inscriptions, have revised the folk tradition and renamed the site Mamallapuram. And it could be so. Mallas have been known in these parts as well as Bali. But we cannot be sure. What is certain is that the Pallavas, who flourished in the area for some 400 years, and were constant rivals to the Pandyas of Madurai, were the builders of the magnificent stone artifacts that remain there.

As my mind went over the story of Bali, I walked towards the left of the granite ridge, and entered a park occupied by five chariots, an elephant and a lion. They are all in stone—creations of the old Pallavas, which are now regarded as being older than the Shore Temple and some of the earliest examples of Dravidian architecture, dating back to the seventh century.

The word "rath", meaning a chariot for carrying an image in procession, is used to describe them, because they are that kind of shape. But there are no stone wheels, such as one sees on the Sun Temple at Konarak, though one could conceive of a real chariot not much smaller than the smallest of them, built of wood rather than stone, and drawn by the elephant that stands beside it.

No doubt they were conceived as such, but the striking thing about them is that they were not built in the normal sense of the word at all. They were excavated. As one stands on the flat ground amongst them, it is difficult to imagine it. Yet, in fact, they were all cut out of massive boulders, first hewn in the rough, then squared up, then cut into to form pillars and tiers of roofs, then chiselled and filed to create the detail of the ornamentation and the reliefs.

This was the method the builders of Mahabalipuram chose to preserve the models of their wooden shrines and living animals in perpetuity, rather than quarrying the stone in some distant place, fashioning it into blocks and pillars, and transporting the pieces to the site to be set up. It is a method that can be seen in its most colossal achievement at Ellora, and in a sense these modest chariots can be regarded as the trial products for that unique creation farther north.

A snake-charmer came up to me, wanting to show me the contest between mongoose and cobra that always reminds me of Rudyard Kipling's Jungle Book. He started blowing into his gourd instrument, making the familiar tremulous, hollow music, and the snake came out of its bag and began to sway its head. A small boy interrupted, begging in five languages—English, German, French, Italian and Russian. It seemed a supreme accomplishment in beggary, even for India.

I left the two of them in order to scramble over the ridge and visit the other old buildings. They are not standing up from the ground, but excavated into the rock, and they must be old too, for here, as on the raths, the Buddhist motifs have not yet quite been ousted by the later Hindu. The centre piece of them all, which is still magnificent although left unfinished, is a large boulder about thirty feet high, almost completely covered with a multitude of carvings in relief.

As amongst the raths, the most conspicuous of the sculptures is a large elephant. He bears witness to the fact that here, too, we are looking at an age when Buddhism and Hinduism were still intermingled, for the prudent, sagacious and loyal elephant was always a symbol of the former faith.

The bull elephant, more than twice the height of a man, has his family with him—a smaller cow behind him and three calves running between his legs—whilst in front of him, but higher up, there is a horribly emaciated man, with his lips drawn back to bare his teeth, and standing on one toe with his hands above his head.

It is after this figure that the rock has been named the Penance of Arjuna, for Arjuna, the hero of the epic Mahabharata, was asked by his brother to propitiate the god Siva by penances and seek the boon of invincibility, since war seemed to be inevitable. He went up into the forests of the Himalayas and practised such severe austerities that the universe was in danger of being burnt up by the energy generated. So Siva decided to grant the boon.

The figure certainly could be Arjuna, but it might equally well be any other ascetic, for there are several others in the relief. There is even a cat playing the ascetic to captivate the mice. The prime motif of the carving is centred elsewhere, on the cleft in the rock that lies between the elephants and the ascetics. It has been cut to represent a river, and in the depths of the cleft, a mermaid-like spirit swims, whilst above her stands the Nag Raja, the snake king, with a halo of cobra hoods.

The dwarfs, flying figures, human beings, lions, monkeys, hares, deer, birds and other animals all look towards the cleft and not towards Arjuna. Below them the elephants face, across the river of stone, a replica of a building like one of the raths down the road, so that there is a repeat, here, of the pattern of the free-standing sculptures. The Descent of the Ganges would be a better title than the Penance of Arjuna.

The sculptured rock still stands there to amaze visitors after twelve centuries, and it is far enough from the sea to have escaped the erosions of time remarkably well. I studied it for a long while, wondering at the innacuracies of guide books, which are misleading as to dimensions and factual detail as well as speculation. Then I went off a short way down the road back to Madras and took the track down to the sea to visit the new tourist bungalow. It was well appointed, and lacked neither service, food nor comforts, contrasting with the guidebook, which as recently as 1962 was recommending the "two-roomed Dak Bungalow: no servants except the watchman, and supplies are difficult to get".

A party of Poles had just arrived, and they were trying to make themselves understood in poor English and worse Hindi. But I did not wish to interfere. After drinking a large lime squash I went out into the heat again and turned the corner for the return to Madras. It was a corner covered with tufts of coarse grass clinging on to the sandy soil, fighting for life in the shrivelling, burning sun. And on it I noticed a group of crude, small crosses and rough headstones.

They were the graves of a little village cemetery, scorched and bare for the nearest tree was in the compound of the bungalow a quarte of a mile away.

So even here, close to the stone monuments of the many-armed gods and goddesses, of the buffalo-headed demon that looks like the Minotaur of Crete, of the boar-headed god Vishnu, of the snake spirits and the river spirits, the simple cross survives. It may have been there before any of those strange creations of the Hindu pantheon were personified, if one doubts not that doubting Thomas came this way.

12

THE HOLY TROGLODYTES

BACK IN Bombay again, now that I am known, I am greeted as a friend. I sit in my air-conditioned room. I drink whisky like a certified alcoholic. I go to the beach hotel at Juhu, bathe and sunbathe, eat prawn curry and drink iced coconut-juice. I do not go beyond the swimming-pool, out of the gate on the seaward side and on to the beach itself, for there the beggars roam, the fortunetellers hunt, the lean children stare, the mangy dogs yap and growl, the monkeys laugh, the excrement lies only just below the surface of the sunbaked sand. I ignore them all, whilst my skin grows thicker every minute of the day. I am learning fast.

Stretched out comfortably beside the pool, I talk to a German, a chemical engineer from Munich, whose firm is helping an Indian company to set up a chemical plant near Trombay, where India's atomic energy centre is located. He tells me the following tale:

On his arrival he was escorted round the embryo chemical plant by the manager, who, with due courtesy, ushered him on ahead into the various departments, calling him "Sir". At a certain point the engineer came to a stopcock. It was badly adjusted, giving a mixture of chemicals in the wrong proportions. Furthermore the operator of the stopcock seemed to have no clear idea of what he was supposed to do, so the German took the stopcock in his own hands, turned it and demonstrated the correct position.

The manager looked on in amazement. The man who had come to advise him on how to run his plant, had actually put his own hand to the wheel. Clearly he was not an executive at all. He was a mere industrial worker. The manager stopped calling him "Sir", and from then on took care to walk in front instead of behind him.

"And you are still staying on?" I asked.

"Yes. Of course I am staying. I have to do the job. But I cannot tell them. They think they know. In every ten metres of piping there are two or three welding leaks. And still they think they know. And these are dangerous substances, highly explosive when they unite."

"I hope you get out alive," I said.

"So do I," the engineer replied. "I want to see Munich again and Garmisch and Berchtesgaden. I don't know whether I shall."

It seemed an unreal fear as we sat and chatted under our orange and white umbrella beside the pool, but I did not think it was. By turning the stopcock himself the engineer had lost caste, and nothing he said to the managerial staff would convince them any more.

I left the swimming-pool and Bombay again to head north-east into a range of hills that were once part of Hyderabad, the dominions of the Nizam. When they were taken from him at the point of the gun in 1948, he was said to be the richest man on earth, yet even at his death in 1967 he was still refusing to pay his taxes, claiming exemption from his electricity bill, and defending his poor contribution to the Prime Minister's Defence Fund after the Chinese invasion by saying that he was a poor man.

Thus the last of the Moguls, as he was often called, left this world to join his ancestors, having spent much and hoarded more, and his state disappeared off the face of the earth with the reorganization of the state boundaries in 1956. The plane delivered me to Aurangabad, where the white marble tomb of the wife of the great Mogul Emperor, Aurangzeb, stands like a miniature Taj Mahal. It is on the outskirts of the city, which was founded by an Abyssinian slave. Eight miles to the west lies Daulatabad, under its huge fortress, and another eight miles along the ridge of hills stands the walled town of Khuldabad, the holy place of the Deccan Muslims. Here Aurangzeb, himself, lies buried, as well as Asaf Jah, the founder of the dynasty that was deposed in 1948 after 200 years.

Old mosques and ruinous mausoleums abound within the walls of Khuldabad, and in them kings, ministers and saints sleep their last long sleep. In one of them there is a garment, which is said to have been actually worn by the Prophet, Mohammed, and in another some hairs of his beard are preserved. It is a quiet place, gently crumbling and collapsing, as the god of destruction works away steadily, like woodworm in the beams of an ancient house.

Another two miles further on a side road plunges down the escarpment towards a wooded plain. It led me away from the

Moguls, back again into the world of Siva and his peers. As my driver took me down the hill, a line of cliffs came into sight on my right. The evening sun was shining full on the rock face, and I could see clearly a row of cave entrances with their carved porches, steps and pathways.

We stopped in a grove of peepul trees opposite a great gap in the cliffs, which seemed to be a central point, for the caves continued on the other side of it to the north. It was even quieter than Khulda-bad, and when the driver switched his engine off, I could distinctly hear the buzzing of bees up in the rocks above.

I walked up to the gap, and found that it was not a natural fault at all. It had been cut out of the cliff face, and in the cutting a great temple had been left standing under the open sky, enclosed on three sides by rock faces equal in height to its topmost tower. The whole complex building and the galleries surrounding it had been carved out of solid rock in a gigantic work, in comparison with which the raths fashioned out of the boulders of Mahabali-puram were puny monuments. It has been estimated that 200,000 tons of volcanic rock must have been cut away to form the halls and pillars and columns of this massive building, and the rock face at the back, which is 100 feet high, shows how deep the excavators must have dug with their simple tools of the eighth century.

I walked in and out of the empty shrines, and in the evening light the over lifesize figures seemed to spring from the rock. Siva's marriage, Siva dancing, Siva the many armed warrior—the impression the sculptors had managed to convey here was one of movement and power rather than sex. The stiffer figures of the earlier days have given place to dynamics in stone. The apsaras fly through the air, the goddesses look down indifferently, absorbed in their own divinity, the gods dance ever on, bestriding the poor world.

Behind this Temple of Heaven, which is the glory of Ellora, a path leads into the cliff. I walked into a cave cut far into the rock, with rows of pillars left to support the roof. Here the effigies were carved on the walls—strange scenes of Siva with a necklace of skulls, Siva springing from a lingam, Siva's marriage again, Vishnu as a dwarf and as a man-lion, Lakshmi and the other Hindu gods and goddesses. They all looked ineffably gloomy and sinister in the dim light, as if in their world all laughter and joy were lost. If one looked long enough, one could see how the thugs, who strangled millions of travellers and stole their possessions, could justify their murders as human sacrifices to Siva's wife.

These caves of the Hindus lie between the earlier Buddhist ones and the later caves of the Jains. They are at the centre of the row of thirty-four caverns, large and small, that are the fruit of cave construction and ornamentation which covers a range of a thousand years. To the south the simpler Buddhist caves lie like a memory of an antique world of modest dignity. To the north the nude saints of the Jains stand in grave, ascetic symmetry, with the jungle creepers, carved in the stone, already climbing up their limbs. Between them lies Siva's world of thrusting power, creating and reproducing, fighting and destroying, held in the dynamic drama of the wheel of life.

And it seemed to me that India was still in Siva's world, and her people were still troglodytes, living in the caves and blind to the world outside. The latest proposals from New Delhi to cope with the desperate population problem sounded like a cry from the very troglodyte heart. Every man was to be sterilized after having three children and given a transistor radio as a reward. The plan was put forward by the health minister, Dr Chandrasekhar, to prevent India producing another Australia in population every year, and the main proposal was reinforced by the suggestion that the minimum age of marriage should be increased from fifteen to twenty and that abortions should be much more generally permitted. But who would man the clinics to carry out the sterilization procedure and the abortions, who would silence the high priests of the Hindus, and who would persuade or command men proud of their virility to submit their bodies to the operation was not defined.

As I drove back to my hotel in Aurangabad, I could not see any hope for India. It seemed like a vast dustbowl of ruins and decrepitude and gnawing poverty, in which the new buildings stood like the rafts of a capsized ship, that would soon be sunk by the mass of survivors struggling in the sea.

My night was disturbed by a mosquito that had got inside my mosquito net and escaped all attempts to locate it, and my morale was far from high when I finally got to sleep. But when I awoke next morning, I sniffed the bright, dry air and the world seemed new again. Was it the scent of the trees, the smell of the earth, or simply the crispness in the atmosphere that took my mind back to the days long years ago when I had learnt to be a soldier tramping the countryside of Mhow?

I drove off again, this time to the north-east, through a lovely peaceful countryside with groves of mango trees in the fields and great deodars shading the road. The harvest was in, and the rich, dark soil was ploughed up again ready for the rain, which must surely come. Handsome Mahratta people passed us by in small groups, some with their blue and red horned cattle. Their women, dressed in rich reds, with long silver pendants in their ears, were working in road gangs in this season between reaping and planting. My spirits lifted to see them look so well, for these people of the fields and pastures were the real stuff of the India the soldiers knew. They were the people who made you welcome in their villages with simple courtesy and gave you unswerving loyalty as long as you kept faith with them.

We drove sixty-five miles till, as at Ellora, the road came down over an escarpment above a wooded plain. It led us round the bend of a dry valley up to the curving cliff face which contains the caves of Ajanta.

I climbed the steep path up to the first cave and looked up at the columns standing across the entrance and at the flying figures on their capitals. It was well-executed, impressive work, but no better than what I had seen already. I was prepared to be disappointed. As soon as I got inside, however, I saw that everything was different. The walls of the cave, that had once been covered all over with coloured paints, still had so much vivid art work on them that my eyes opened wide in wonder.

At the far end of the cave there was a great statue of the Buddha, seated with his hands in the teaching position. On either side of him stood Bodhisattvas in their golden crowns and coloured loin cloths. White pearls glowed with an almost phosphorescent light against the dark skin of carefully coiffured women. One panel tells the tale of an embassy from Persia, another illustrates the story of the Buddha's temptation by Mara, and a third relates the tale of the king who saved a pigeon from a hawk by offering up its weight in his own flesh. Monkeys jump about in the corners and peacocks show off their green and blue tails.

In these earlier caves of Ajanta a whole world, which had died at Ellora, seemed to me to come to life again. The ochre and the vegetable green, the red and the white and the lamp black, and the

13

blue that was probably imported from Persia, combine in these wonderful coloured survivals of the past, which are so rare because of the perishable nature of pigments, to give us a glimpse of how the artists of ancient India viewed the world. This, we can say, is the sort of work that Indians were doing when Christ was born, and if the beauty of the figures and the calm and compassionate expressions on their faces are anything to go by, it was a nobler vision than the one that Siva dominated in later times.

Yet for a thousand years the caves remained hidden behind a screen of fallen rock and vegetation, until in 1819 they were discovered accidentally. Sixteen years after the nearby walled town of Ajanta had been commandeered by Wellesley to accommodate the wounded after he had defeated the Mahrattas at the battle of Assaye an officer of the East India Company was out hunting on the plateau overlooking the Wagora valley. He gazed across at the opposite cliff, and there was a section of it that seemed to form a pattern that was too regular in shape to be a natural formation. It was a part of the façade of one of the caves. Closer investigation was followed by the removal of the rubble and the revelation of the hidden glory within.

Twenty-five years later Major Gill commenced a labour of love that lasted nearly twenty years. He copied the most striking frescoes in oils and took them home with him to England, only to have a large number of them destroyed in the fire at the Crystal Palace exhibition of 1866. Since then other copies of the paintings have been done, and latterly a complete photographic record has been made. Yet it was Major Gill who first showed their beauties to the world, and it was fitting that it should have been so, for it was men like him, who worked in and for India, and loved the land and its people, and brought order out of chaos with the army that they trained, who should be remembered.

As I returned to Aurangabad along the quiet country road I thought of Major Gill, and of the other army men who had lived in India and loved it. They were mostly straightforward men of good will, who would talk to a peasant about his land and his crops, help him where possible and go hunting, shooting and fishing like the country squires back home. And these were the people the Indian country folk could accept and like for their honesty and fair-dealing and the security they brought to their lives. When the time came for those forthright, hearty figures in khaki shorts and shirts to leave, there were many who were deeply sorry to see them go.

Even when I got back to Bombay and the city life, something remained of the love for India that my visit to Ajanta had revived. It was good to leave with the balance in the love-hate relationship restored, to see the good things as well as the hopelessness, and to remember the treks in the Himalayas and the quiet content of an evening on the veranda of a dak bungalow after a hot day's march as well as the slums of the cities and the tongue-twisting politicians. The final word was with the middle-aged man, incongruously dressed in a creased white dhoti, whom I saw on my return to the super hygienic affluence of Zürich's new airport building. He was sitting on one of the side benches of the shiny new passenger lounge, with one leg cocked up underneath the other, gazing dreamily into space with that inward Indian look in his eyes that always makes one wonder what is going on behind them. "I am going back to India," he said. "I am going home."

INDEX

INDEX